THE FLOW
Africa's Rising Tide

by

Rodwell Jacha
2020

evolve

PUBLICATIONS

Evolve Publications: info@evolvepublications.co.za
Special Sales: +27 79 670 7829 or jacha@moving-ads.co.za
Manufactured in the Republic of South Africa
Executive Publisher: Edwin Ngoni Tawengwa
Editor: Kennedy Mpezeni
Typesetting: Winston Tshili of Infinity Multimedia
Artwork/Cover: Mehluli Hikwa

Unless otherwise indicated, all Scriptures references are from the King James Version of the Holy Bible.

ISBN 978-0-620-86897-6

ACKNOWLEDGEMENTS

Above all thank you to the Champion of Champions, King of Kings, the One who saved me and changed the flow of my life, Jesus Christ my Saviour and the Saviour of the world.

What would an author do without a host of dedicated professional friends? I owe a great debt of gratitude to my brothers in Christ, Edwin Tawengwa and Kennedy Mpezeni for working tirelessly in assisting with the research and editorial work that this work demanded and the most special people who prayed for the project.

My wife Nthombikayise and our amazing family whose patience I have always coveted, in letting me do what I was called to do while sacrificing their time.

TABLE OF CONTENTS

"Flow"

intransitive verb…

(1): to issue or move in a stream
(2): circulate
(3) Movement of currency
(4) Direction
(5) The place of convergence
b: to move with a continual change of place
c: to proceed "from"
2: rise
3: abound
4a: to proceed smoothly and readily
b: to have a smooth continuity

INTRODUCTION

—∞—

"ex Africa semper aliquid novi"
"Out of Africa there is always something new"
Gaius Plinius Secundus aka Pliny the Elder

There are many stories told about Africa. Stories told by people who have no direct connection to her. These narratives are told through the biased lenses of people who are unfamiliar with the true pulse of the African heartbeat. They have no roots, presence, or experience, of what it means to be African and yet they dare speak conclusively on Africa's behalf.

These voices dominate the channels that tell corrupted versions of our story as though we have no voice of our own. The result has been a distorted view and perception of Africa, her history, economic landscape, future, destiny, wealth, and people.

Who else can tell the African story better than the African? A paradoxical story characterised by complexity, superstition, distortion, hope, and promise. A tale of a people once enslaved and oppressed but now liberated and free. Sadly, only our dark and dreary ages dominate the present storyline of our continent and their shadows are being cast as an interpretation of our future and destiny. Yet there has been a magnanimous paradigm-shift in Africa's trajectory. A shift that has its genesis in the mind of our Creator. The titanic continent has been changing course, and many have missed the memo because we have become so attuned to history that we have become oblivious to her eminent destiny.

We must tell our own story and set the record straight. It is time we reclaim our voice and our convoluted history of adversity, exploitation, and rape. We need to recast our story from the perspective of the God who created Africa and the African. It is time that we tune in to the mind of God, and locate his original plans and intentions for the Motherland and tell our narrative as one of triumph over adversity and a defiant victory over the forces that have sought to arrest our progress. A story of hope, promise, and a brighter future. The true African story.

Confronting the Dark Continent Myth

While Africa has a controversial history, the beloved continent is not its past. We must cease to be defined by the condescending Eurocentric conclusions that conceal the role Europe played in paralysing our continent. In the same breath, we must refuse to be a project of donor aid and we must desist from engaging the world seeking the pity of philanthropic paternalism. Instead, we must return to our tried and tested systems that promoted frank, honest, and progressive dialogue among ourselves as reflected in the *indabas* (gatherings of our wisest sages) of our ancient kingdoms. We need to have a conversation that will define and articulate our challenges and the solutions we so desperately need to successfully align our continent to the seasons of the Father. Africa must take ownership of her destiny and more importantly, she must take responsibility for redefining her future.

What A Time to be African

These are exciting times to be an African. The African who will wear a new lens will own the future. A paradigm shift is an absolute necessity in these times. Once this shift takes place, the Africans will be empowered to create a new future for themselves and their fellow kinfolk. As this new season dawns over the continent God has been raising game-changers all over Africa. Men and women who are bringing change and transformation to households, communities, cities, nations, economies, and the world. Men and women like prolific inventor Moses Musaazi of Uganda whose company, *Technology for Tomorrow* creates Africa-relevant innovative solutions such as the interlocking stabilised soil blocks made using ordinary non-organic soil, a small amount of cement and a little water. These bricks are stronger than fired bricks, can be made on site and have been used successfully to build houses, water tanks and granaries. Out of Kenya, we have seen Beth Koigi, whose company Majik Water, invented a technology that harvest water from air, something that drought prone regions will benefit from.

God placed us on this blessed continent for a time such as this and we are returning to the days when Africans walked on this planet as the envy of all. We are going back to our rightful place of dominion over the continent and its resources to the glory of God and the service of humanity, and not just a privileged few. Unfortunately, this is not the case yet. It is not yet *uhuru* on the continent. We still have some deep work to do. We need to dislodge the many ancient ideologies that have dominated our collective psyche and rescript the narrative that we believe about Africa. The old and self-sabotaging patterns of thought that we had bought into as Africans, are responsible for our present state and we must rid ourselves of them. Our young Africans cannot continue to dream of escaping the source from which most of the flows that fuel the global economy originates. We cannot allow future generations to deal with the frustrations born from a perceived lack of opportunity that is untrue and rooted in the frameworks of the colonial and post-independence era of Africa.

A new day has dawned over Africa. God is doing a new thing and we must perceive it (Isaiah 40:31). We must be willing to challenge the narratives we have believed throughout the ages and see things differently, from the Father's perspective. God has blessed Africa with so much abundance it is mind-blowing and yet our youth continue to leave our shores in pursuit of greener pastures in Europe, Asia, and America. And yet the mighty flow that has built those economies is rooted on the very same African soil that they are fleeing from. This narrative is shifting, and Africa's tide is rising. It is now time that Africa and the African position themselves to ride the tide.

God's Prophetic Promise

Scripture is pregnant with so much unfulfilled prophecy concerning Africa. One such word is *"Princes shall come out of Egypt; Ethiopia shall soon stretch her hands unto the Lord"* (Psalms 68:13). This prophetic promise gives hope that a brighter day awaits us. Africa will have princes flowing out of her; young men and women of vision who will bless the nations with their ideas, innovations, and solutions. We are seeing this prophetic word manifest before our very eyes as young men and women of African origin and descent emerging and making waves in various spheres of global influence.

Africa's hands are also being stretched towards the Lord, as our worship flows towards the King of Kings from the hearts of a grateful and God-fearing people. Africans of all nations, cultures, languages, tribes, race, and domicile are raising their hands and voices in worship to the Almighty like no other ethnicity on the planet. Sadly, this is far from the picture that is painted about us. All that is ever magnified is what the evil one has perpetrated on our soil - despotic leadership, poverty, hunger, infant mortality, corruption, witchcraft, and ethnic conflict. Little to no attention is given to the contribution to the world by Africa and Africans. Think of the spiritual revival taking place on the continent, the millions who are coming to the Lord annually, and our indigenous African churches are sending missionaries who are turning the developed world upside down with the gospel of Jesus Christ. Our many emerging economies that are registering some of the highest growth rates in the world, the improvement of governance and transparency, Africans who are innovating in technological spaces, peaceful democratic transitions in the majority of our states, rising literacy rates, expansion of social services to include more and more of our people and so much more.

God's hand is upon Africa and something is turning, and things are taking shape and coming into alignment with his times, seasons, and purposes for Africa. We must, as a matter of urgency, rise from our slumber and prepare ourselves for what God is doing in this season. We must acquire the knowledge, wisdom, understanding, and enlightenment necessary to operate and function in sync with these exciting times. We must be ready to make the changes, realignments, and adaptations necessary for us to catch the wave of the rising tide and change our fortunes forever. Like the sons of Issachar, we ought to understand these prophetic times we live in and know what to do.

The Significance of Africa

"And a river went out of Eden to water the garden, and from thence it was parted, and became into four heads.
The name of the first is Pison: that is, it which compasseth the whole land of Havilah, where there is gold.
And the gold of that land is good: there is bdellium and the onyx stone.
And the name of the second river is Gihon: the same is it that compasseth the whole land of Ethiopia.
And the name of the third river is Hiddekel: that is, it which goeth toward the east of Assyria. And the fourth river is Euphrates."

Genesis 2:10 – 14

When God placed man in the garden, there was a river that flowed into Eden and watered the garden, and there were four rivers that flowed out of Eden. The flow into Eden was designed to ensure that the garden was well irrigated, fertile and that Adam's productivity was constantly at peak. His level of productivity was governed by his ability to manage the flow that irrigated the garden. It is this flow that would nourish his fields and make his efforts fruitful. The presence of the flow did not guarantee the fruitfulness of the garden. Adam had to channel the river that flowed into the garden for Eden to flourish. What a tragedy it would have been if the rivers that flowed out of Eden were responsible for ensuring that territories beyond the garden were adequately supplied with the flow of Eden but Eden itself being desolate. Such a reality would expose ignorance, incompetence, and negligence on the part of Adam.

God positioned Adam in the place where the flow sprung to teach Adam a principle, which if we were to grasp as Africa, our destiny and narrative will change dramatically for the good. This principle is what I call the blessing of the flow.

The Blessing of the Flow

"Wherever the river flows, there will be many fish and animals. The river will make the water in the Dead Sea fresh. Wherever the river flows, it will bring life."

Ezekiel 47:9

(GOD's WORD Translation)

There is power and blessing in a flow. Flows signify life, movement, and activity. Whenever there is stagnation, there is death but wherever there is a flow there is life and freshness. Medically death begins when the heart ceases to pump blood to the vitals and other parts of the body. When the flow stops, life ceases. Economically, we express economic growth and development in terms of the circulation and flow of money. When the flow slows down, we have a recession and in certain cases depression. Electrically, we appreciate that power is only existent when there is a flow of current. When the flow stops, there is no power.

Flows are valuable assets and the whole world seems to appreciate the importance and the blessing of the flows that springs forth from our Great Continent. Therefore, the world's superpowers are at war with each other as they scramble for Africa's flow. The world is cannibalising itself, as brother turns against brother because of the desperation created by greed and selfishness in pursuit of the flows. The world's economic titans are manoeuvring as they step over each other to take over the flows of the Great Continent of Africa. This is happening before our very eyes. Sadly, we the African people are shamefully divided and are ignorantly facilitating the acceleration of the scramble and parcelling out of our wealth to the rest of the world, even though we are being excluded from the blessings of the flow under our stewardship.

Politicians rig elections, rebel leaders commit heinous crimes, our nations are ablaze in tension and conflict, terrorist groups abduct and rape our daughters and militarise our sons, and innocent lives are devastated as entire groups are suppressed and marginalised. This happens only because an elite few seek to control the flows of our continent's wealth, ideas, power, and ultimate destiny at the expense of the continent and its people.

There is Good News

The good news is that the all-wise God made it possible for us to transcend all this pettiness that we witness all over Africa. He has created more than enough resources for all who are living now and those who are yet unborn to exploit and enjoy. Our responsibility is to manage the flow as faithful stewards of what He has entrusted us with. We are to pass on a better continent than the one we inherited. Future generations are looking to us to change the narrative and the flow. He promises that He will make us rulers over much when we are faithful with little. It is time that we as African people begin to value ourselves, our fellow Africans, our land, our legacy, our inheritance, our portion, and our flows. We must develop astuteness of stewardship and prove ourselves faithful as a generation so that God will bless our posterity with an abundance because of us. This is a challenge which requires wisdom and insight on our part because the only way to ensure that the flow serves the purpose God created it for is to change how we view and appreciate the flow and make the necessary adjustments so we can **CHANGE THE FLOW!**

The Power of Unity

"And the LORD said, Behold, the people is one, and they have all one language; and this they begin to do: and now nothing will be restrained from them, which they have imagined to do."

Genesis 11:6

To transform the continent from the present state of desolation to the peak of her potential a new and unifying vision for our future needs to be articulated and cast. A vision of shared prosperity that is built on a new narrative that speaks possibilities and not our dark and dreary past. The story of Nimrod gives us an appreciation of the power of this principle. Firstly, we learn the importance of vision in unifying people. Nimrod was able to unify mankind through the power of a compelling and inclusive vision. From the language used in Scripture, we can discern that the idea was one that was held by all. *"Come, let us..."*. It is evident that though he may have cast the vision it was embraced by all.

Secondly, they were able to find agreement because they spoke the same language. This is something Africa needs to learn. We cannot continue to operate at cross purposes and compete against each other and expect to progress. If we desire progress and development, we must start speaking one language as a people. We must do away with speaking impossibilities and start to speak what can be. When we speak one language, we understand each other, and this improves our ability to connect, collaborate, and coordinate ourselves under the one vision we share. It is impossible to unify people who do not share a common vision and common language. It is time we learn to sing from the same hymn book as Africans. Our nationalities, races, tribes, political ideologies, social and economic classes, religious preferences, and whatever else we may allow to divide us must never take centre stage. We need to find common ground as a people and build on that. We already share common challenges like poverty, inequality, a colonial past, and limited access to opportunity. Instead of fighting around what divides us, we can come and dialogue around the issues that we have in common and develop a vision of shared prosperity for all.

When we unite and choose unity over division, we not only experience God's commanded blessing, but nothing we imagine will ever be impossible to us. The season is not one to be fighting but we should be working together to capture the flow and build our illustrious future as a continent and a people.

DEDICATION

To all the Leaders who have and are speaking and standing to raise the previously disadvantaged people groups in our world.

PREFACE

Everyone who sat at the table was hungry. They all came with insatiable appetites. Each thinking about their bellies as they began to engage each other in discourse. They all knew what they had come to the table for. They had come to dine and eat to their heart's content. They came to eat as much as they could and then some more. After they were satiated, they proceed to loot the dinner table for their posterity and nations. Not everyone would get an equal share on this table nor was anyone concerned about this sore fact and truth. None cared about the goose that had laid the golden eggs they were all-consuming voraciously without restraint. As for the host, they consumed the crumbs and were left to clean up the mess.

This is the story of Africa. It has been her narrative for centuries.

"There is a tide in the affairs of men, which taken at the flood, leads on to fortune. Omitted, all the voyage of their life is bound in shallows and in miseries. On such a full sea are we now afloat. And we must take the current when it serves or lose our ventures."

Julius Caesar

PART I

THE FLOW

CHAPTER ONE

THE AFRICAN SPRING

—⌀⌀—

"Joy comes in spring"

The Spring Has Sprung

When the winter season has dragged for long and its low hanging dark grey clouds linger in a deceitful way that extends its welcome, the human heart becomes weary and desperate, longing for a new season to break forth. For after all who loves winter more than they do spring. Few people like the cold. In winter things shrivel, wilt, and die. But spring always comes with promise. It sets in with the hope of recovering all that had been lost during the austere winter season.... Despite the severity of winter, spring always comes, and with it a new season of blooming and blossoming... Spring is beautiful...

Spring is here. Thank God! It signals much needed change, and it spells a new beginning and trajectory. While it may not represent the full effect of the change, spring signals the genesis of the new. Africa has entered her season of spring. Turnaround is here. Dawn has broken and a new day is emerging. The tide is rising, and the environment is opening. Africa is ripe for business and open for the new thing that God is doing. The motherland's spiritual womb is fertile and ready to bring forth. There have been so many changes but in this season of spring, Africa is in a time of reform and transition. We are a continent in shift. And this shift is carrying us from a lower status into our rightful place of respect and recognition. It is time for the African spring.

"I will open rivers in high places, and fountains in the midst of the valleys: I will make the wilderness a pool of water, and the dry land springs of water."
Isaiah 41:18

Not only is spring a season, it is a fountain too. This makes it a source of hope. From it, new and fresh possibilities proceed. A spring has the power to turn a parched and dry desert into a bubbly ecosystem that can sustain and support livelihoods, communities, industries, nations, continents, and the globe. Springs nourish and water potential, hopes, dreams, and aspirations. The presence of a spring opens so many avenues for the transformation of even the most lifeless and desolate of places. It is no surprise that when Scriptures speaks of a prosperous and righteous man, it speaks of him as being planted by the rivers. This indicates that he is always fresh and flourishing in and out of season, and fruitful in its season because he is planted by the springs or the rivers (Psalms 1:5). This should be our portion as Africa. We should be flourishing and fruitful because we are in our season of spring and we are a spring.

When Spring Breaks Forth

December 17, 2010 will go down as a defining moment in the destiny of North Africa. It was an ordinary day in the calendar of Tunisia. No one would have imagined that a new path would be charted that day. A street vendor by the name Mohammed Bouazizi, had been going about his daily routine before an altercation with the state's oppressive police over the arbitrary seizure of his vegetable stand inspired him to set himself ablaze in protest. His act ignited a revolution within the dominantly Arab North Africa. Mohammed act sparked what has come to be referred to by analysts as the Arab Spring, as it led to a major shift in the power dynamic within the predominantly Muslim North, which saw major authoritarian regimes dislodged. It was named the Arab Spring by political scientist Marc Lynch in his article in Foreign Policy, a political science journal. He used this term to liken what was happening in North Africa and the Middle East, to the Prague revolutions of 1968. In this context the spring is viewed on two major levels, the season when a nation or people are ripe and ready for change, and the gushing forth of something new, as a spring would in a dry and desert place. Just as the Arab Spring spouted forth unexpectedly, another spring is breaking forth before our very eyes; it is what I call the African Spring.

The African Spring refers to the *"kairos"* season dawning over Africa and her people where our continent is beginning to bud, bloom, and blossom. We are coming into our own. The veil of lies that had been placed over our eyes has begun to disintegrate like chaff and our eyes are beginning to open to our potential and the boundless possibilities before us. Unlike our predecessors who were intimidated by the gunships, rifles, and the horsemanship of the colonisers of yesteryear, and saw themselves as inferior, young Africans from all over the world are emerging and seeing themselves as equals in the global village and economy. They appreciate that Africa's value to the world can never be overstated. They understand just how capable, competent, and critical they are to the bigger picture of global advancement, prosperity, and development. And they are demanding their seat at the table. Spring has sprung on the continent. A new day has dawned, and the African is ready to business with the world.

The African Spring also refers to the untapped wealth flowing through Africa, represented by the minerals, land, wildlife, knowledge, skills, competencies, innovations, and anything that is indigenous to Africa and can be a blessing to the world. In this season we are realising a truth that has been hidden from us for generations. Africa is the spring that has always irrigated the global economy. We are the source of the global flows that have built the world economy as we know it. We are the spring and the fountain from which these flows spout and nourish the rest of the world. Whether we are speaking of mineral wealth, human capital, spirituality, and agricultural produce, all these flow from our blessed continent to the world. Africa is pivotal to global growth and development as we are a strategic supplier of natural resources, a huge and growing consumer market, a pool of young talent, a thriving and growing church, and the next frontier for economic emergence. Africa is open for harvest and the motherland is open for business.

The Renewable Spring

From the moment the African spring was created by our God, a flow was born which can never be stopped or shut off. A natural spring is born when underground water capitalises on a vulnerability within the earth, and it pushes itself to the earth's surface with a volcanic-like force at very high pressure. As this flow surges through these cracks, it widens the conduit to allow greater volumes to gush forth without restraint. The torrential force of this underground flow propels the water above the earth's surface before it settles in the immediate environment, where it forms a basin, and there its surface level flow is initiated. In geography, they refer to this point as the source of the river. Driven by the perpetual flow emanating from the gushing fountain, the water begins to follow the path of least resistance; navigating through the contours of nature, and meandering around stubborn obstacles, it begins to gather momentum as it continues to find its way. Suddenly everything around it begins to support its movement as it hastens its journey to wherever it is needed and valued most.

The law of gravity also kicks in and adds velocity to this flow, the trees, rocks, and other barriers go from being impediments to catalysts, as they too accelerate the current of the river as it increases its influence, before it empties itself into a bigger river, lake, sea, or ocean. This it does continually without cessation. The volumes and the velocity may differ in their measures following nature's calendar, but the flow itself never stops.

Sounds Like the Motherland

The analogy above relates very well with the motherland, Africa. As Africans we find ourselves living on the fountain of all major global flows. Even in our modern era, Africa continues to discover new springs of wealth, ideas, innovation, and resources that the world is craving after. From the liquified petroleum gas and oil reserves recently discovered in Mozambique and Ghana, the recent discovery of uranium and diamonds in Zimbabwe, the fertile soils known for the finest cocoa production in the Ivory Coast, and the innovative mobile money transfer solutions developed in Kenya, there has been a growing global demand for what Africa's soil, her people, and their ideas have to offer. These and many such sightings have brought about an unprecedented awakening of global interest in our continent. The fact is undisputed that we are the richest continent of them all. God has placed an abundance of wealth under our feet in the form of arable land, hinterlands that are rich with diamonds, oil, gold, platinum, and so much more. Our urban areas are populated by a young, talented, agile, tech-savvy, and driven demographic that is diligent and competent. We are the envy of the world. Therefore, every other continent wants a share in the African cake because of its unending flows.

The Scramble for the Flow

We are the spring of the flow that the global economy relies heavily upon. The world's superpowers are constantly at loggerheads over our continent, as they work tirelessly to try and take control of the abundant flows of our great Africa, so they can channel them to their favour. So much flow is generated within Africa annually. Resources, revenue, skills, ideas, and indigenous technology are constantly being extracted out of this beautiful continent. The sad part is that all these extracts exit our shores with very little, if any, benefit accruing to our people, communities, economies, and states.

Historically, we have many cases of the world scrambling to harness our flows. Our blood, sweat, and tears along with significant amounts of our gold, platinum, and oil, so many of our scholars, innovators, and creatives, and our wisdom and intellectual property have been constantly emptying themselves into the ocean of the global economy, where they have been redirected to Europe, Asia, Oceania, and the Americas. Places where these mega flows were systematically captured and then intentionally integrated into their channels and used in building those economies and states into economic titans and superpowers that they are today. The same superpowers then turn around and sell us the value-added products they made from our resources, both natural and human, at a cost far higher than what we earned for the for our export of the same raw materials.

In our contemporary times, we have seen new entrants enter the scramble to harness our flows to their favour. Asia, the Middle East and emerging economies of South America are all deepening their interest in the African economy through investment and trade, and the strengthening of diplomatic and economic ties with Africa. As global interest in our flows intensifies, the various strategic efforts by the many investor nations are being realigned to ensure that they have a greater grip of the flows of Africa's resources.

This then begs the question, since Africa is so pivotal, where is her benefit in all this? Since we are as critical to the global economy as we are, how come we are so peripheral in the industries and the global affairs that our soil and people support? Is it because we are always getting raw deals regardless of whether we engage East or West as partners in development? Why do we contribute so much and yet we benefit the least? Is it because we sit at the table negotiating as desperados who will take any deal that comes even if it does not work in our favour? What can we do differently so we can catch the rising tide and turn our captivity? What new skills, sensitivities, and approaches must we adopt going forward? Do we need to engage the international community from the perspective of an entrepreneur wooing investors by focusing on creating win/win outcomes that work for us as well as for them? Whatever it is that we must do, Africa needs to change and realign and make sure that the spring, Africa, is benefitting first and foremost from the rich flows it initiates and channels to the rest of the world. We must ensure that is she is not being raped incessantly and left weak and in ruins, desolate, and underdeveloped, as she perpetually contributes to the accelerated growth of the rest of the world to her demise. We must equally ensure that investor capital is safe and secure on our continent by ensuring peace, security, and stability. We need to commit to building the institutions that will strengthen our states and safeguard us from the many political, economic, social, regional, continental, and global shocks that are prevalent in these disruptive times. We must also commit to an uninterrupted developmental trajectory. We must also make it easier for money to enter and exit our shores. Our investment markets should not feel like prisons when they are an African paradise that is flowing with milk and honey.

CHAPTER TWO

THIS IS AFRICA

—✺—

"A Land Flowing with Milk and Honey"
Danny: *"Peace Corps types only stay around long enough to real-
ize they're not helping anyone. Governments only want to stay in
power until they've stolen enough to go into exile somewhere else.
And the rebels, they are not sure they want to take over. Other-
wise, they would have to govern this mess. But TIA."*
Maddie: *"What's TIA?"*
Danny: *"This Is Africa."*
~Quote from the Movie, Blood Diamond

Before I become overly excited about the rise of this sleeping
giant called Africa, let me summarise the intrigue of her back-
ground. A plethora of names have been used to refer to her; some
became popular, while others are long forgotten. One name given
to Africa that has stood out over the centuries is *"The Dark Continent."* This name may have been brought about because the nar-
rator had very little knowledge about the continent, or they may
have concluded that her inhabitants were not so clever, or it was
about the dominant skin colour of her people, or it was based on
the gross underdevelopment of the continent. Another school of
thought can be traced back to the missionaries who referred to us
by that term because they believed that the continent was domi-

nated by the demonic forces of the dark underworld. The list of probabilities is endless, but the truth behind that lie is this, they called us the *"Dark Continent"* because for ages we have been ignorant of the flows that we have been blessed with on this land. We were clueless regarding the value and volume of what lies under our feet. For generations, we had no idea that the flows of the resource we have coursing through Africa, are responsible for developing the mega economies of the world to where they are today. The tragedy was that not only were the natural resources extracted out of the continent for a song, they flowed out of Africa without adding value to the continent, its people, economies, and communities. It was not long before the pennies we realised from selling our raw materials followed suit, and so did the human capital and all its inherent potential. All flowing into the global economy at Africa's expense.

However, God has opened the eyes and minds of His people to realise who they are and whose they are. Africans are beginning to appreciate what is theirs by Divine birth right. We are rediscovering our pride, identity, and dignity. The unfailing love of God the Father has awakened the realisation that God is calling the African child to become a better custodian and steward of the flows they have been blessed with by God.

The Times Are Ours

As we respond to this *"zeitgeist"* of our times, we need leaders from all spheres to emerge who will call Africa to attention, so we can reform and restructure our lives, enterprises, industries, institutions, economies, policies, and states to ensure that we grow into more proficient stewards of the streams that flow throughout our continent. We need leaders who like Joseph, can manage the flows during the years of plenty, to ensure abundant supply in times of famine. In so doing, Joseph propelled Egypt into a becoming a superpower by managing the flows with finesse.

The times demand that we shift with them. It cannot be business as usual on the continent. It is time for business unusual. In these times we must operate with a deeper sense of enlightenment and understanding that we were never the *"Dark Continent."* Since time immemorial we have always been a people whose hearts and minds have always been illuminated. We just simply need to go back into history to appreciate this.

The Spiritual Flow

As early as the days of the Apostles in the book of Acts, an Ethiopian eunuch, who served as an official in the court of Queen Candace, was reading a portion of Scripture from the book of Isaiah. He needed assistance to understand what he was reading. Effectively demonstrating that our people have been intellectually inclined for ages, but that is not my focus here. The eunuch went on to receive the Lord Jesus Christ as Lord and Saviour and was baptised. According to the <u>Church Father</u>, <u>St. Irenaeus</u> of Lyons in his book <u>*Adversus haereses*</u> *(Against the Heresies*, an early anti-<u>gnostic</u> theological work) (180 AD), wrote regarding the Ethiopian eunuch, *"This man (<u>Simeon Bachos the Eunuch</u>) was also sent into the regions of Ethiopia, to preach what he had himself believed, that there was one God preached by the prophets, but that the Son of this (God) had already made (His) appearance in human flesh, and had been led as a sheep to the slaughter; and all the other statements which the prophets made regarding Him."* This shows that the gospel came to the continent long before the missionaries did. We do not owe our faith in the Lord to them in any way. Yes, they renewed our consciousness of the Living God, for history shows that somewhere along the line we had adulterated our worship.

Africa's flow is not only economic. It is also deeply spiritual. The impact the indigenous African church has had on the global spiritual landscape testifies to this. The African church is registering more salvations annually and planting more churches globally than any other continental church. This phenomenon is not new, people from the continent have always been engaged with the God of heaven and earth, be it here on the African soil or wherever they were held as slaves in Europe or America. After many years of unnoticed suffering, God in His faithfulness began to show His people that they were not alone and that He had not forgotten them. From the very same oppressed slaves, scientists began to emerge. Such truths would be suppressed, but the truth cannot be hidden forever. In the movie *"Hidden Figures"* we are told of three brilliant African women whose ancestors died as slaves in America and had served as the brains behind one of the greatest operations in history: the launch of astronaut Colonel John Glenn (Glenn Powell) into orbit, a stunning achievement that restored confidence to America during the space race. The three African American women were Katherine Johnson (Taraji P Henson) Dorothy Vaughan (Octavia Spencer) and Mary Jackson (Janelle Monae). Despite the oppression they faced, they never lost their faith in God and they continued to seek Him in prayer and worship.

The children of African slaves rose from the ashes as a result of the powerful spiritual outflow born in prayer. Many other unsung heroes who are among the greatest inventors are Garrett Morgan, who invented a hair-straightening chemical; George Washington Carver, who made important agricultural discoveries and inventions; Lewis Howard Latimer, an African inventor who improved on Edison's light bulb; Shirley Jackson, who was responsible for the breakthrough research that led to the invention of the fibre-optic cable and other communication technologies; Marie Van Brittan Brown, a nurse who together with her husband developed a home security system; Otis Boykin, an engineer, who invented the control unit for an artificial cardiac pacemaker. The list goes on and on, but the point I am making is when slaves were being treated like animals, none of the so-called masters ever thought that the hidden treasure in these people of God will rise again.

These achievements are not restricted to the African Diaspora, even right here on the continent we have our people achieving so many exploits like M-pesa a global mobile money transfer platform developed in Kenya, and Lokole, an innovation which was developed in the Democratic Republic of Congo, which allows for data access in remote areas and provides remote medical and educational assistance to rural DRC. These innovations were functional and operational on the continent of Africa long before the covid-19 pandemic. God has blessed our people as He did the Midianites with foresight and insight to prepare for the future ahead of time. The same way he prepared Egypt for a time of famine by giving Joseph the wisdom and strategy to build strategic reserves when abundance was flowing. Now, this is the real African narrative!

Dispelling the African Myth

Western media has portrayed an image of Africa as a disease-infested, and poverty-stricken land populated by confused barbarians. We were branded the *"Dark Continent"* by people who had their motives. Unfortunately, this came with such negative energy that many African people began to believe this lie. This can become a big debate, but I think we have issues of greater gravity to deal with than focusing on the trivial details. Now, as the future unfolds before us, we need to step up and begin to build our African brand correctly and prophetically. I am convinced that the most authentic people on the planet are found on the African continent. The atmosphere on this continent is such that we cannot help but be real with ourselves and our neighbours. One of the contributing factors is the dominance of the Christian faith on the continent; we are grateful to the Lord for sending missionaries from all over the planet, the British and Americans in particular. They revived our faith in God and reignited our passion for the gospel and we say God bless them. We are even more grateful that today the African church has taken lead in global missions and is the one sending missionaries to the rest of the world. The tide has truly turned.

This charming continent needs to be rebranded to reflect the truth about its past, present, and future reality. A beautiful continent endowed with ever-smiling and hardworking people whose voices are so melodious that you would be forgiven to think they cannot speak but can only sing, ought to be known as such by the rest of the world. In Africa, our people do not just walk – they have a dance in every step. When our people choose to dance, you would be forgiven to think they are made of rubber with the way they swing their bodies. Sadly, this is not how we have been perceived by the world and more painfully by ourselves.

Changing Our Narrative

From Mount Kilimanjaro to the Atlas Mountains, down to the Rwenzori Mountains and the Zambezi valley, every mountain range tells a story of its people and the rich wildlife we were blessed with. Every lake, river, bushveld, desert, and waterfall all tell a rich story about our continent. Our environs are blessed with abundant resources that God deposited under our feet for our blessing and exploitation in serving Him and advancing humanity. These resources are either being extracted, explored, processed, preserved, or they are yet to be discovered. The so-called rare earth minerals are rare to the rest of the world, but to Mother Africa, they are as common as stones. The world has no clue what is about to be emerge from this sleeping giant!

I for one, am proud enough to stick my chest out and say the future of the world is housed in this beautiful gem, the African continent. The most exciting truth is that children of the continent are rising with such majesty that one cannot help but to be proud with humility as we witness the glory of God upon a people who were once oppressed and subjugated. As He promised Solomon when he dedicated the temple, God is bringing healing and transformation to our land, He is restoring us to our dignity and our place of prominence in the community of nations. *"If my people who are called by my name, shall humble themselves, pray and seek my face and turn from their wicked ways, and then I will hear from heaven, and will heal their land"* (2 Chronicles 7: 14). Africa is in her season of healing and restoration. The narrative of the so-called curse is being corrected before our very eyes.

Africa Rising

Africa, it is time to rise and be proud of who you are! It is said, *"history repeats itself"*. This is a very true saying. Civilisation has its roots and genesis in Africa and the whole world perfected what was originated on this continent. Math, language, engineering, and art all began on the continent and now, a completely new industrial revolution is about to be launched in Africa and the world will once again come and take notes from us.

In rebranding our beautiful continent, we do not need to do much because for decades the bad publicity was topical news for the entire world. All things bad, such as diseases, wars, and even natural disasters were only *"happening"* on the African continent. If people get used to knowing that nothing good comes out of Africa and suddenly, they hear of the good that God is doing here, they might dismiss it at first, but the more good news they hear, they will eventually stop and listen. After listening, they might still doubt, but those who will dig for more information, will eventually see the truth and be liberated from the false narratives that have been pushed about our amazing continent. We need to arise and use who we are, as great and yet contrite-hearted people and tell our stories.

For a long time, our stories have been narrated and misinterpreted by those who were quick and zealously eager to tell our stories without understanding. Thank God the flow has changed; we have now begun to tell our own stories. All one needs to do is go on to sites like Ted.com, YouTube, or attend the World Economic Forum in Davos or Cape Town, the Global Entrepreneurship Summit in Nairobi, Kenya, and the talks at Chatham House where Africans have courageously begun to set the record straight. These platforms have gone a long way to correcting the falsehoods and negative stereotypes held about our people and continent. On there you will find stories of peaceful and progressive transfer of power, accelerated economic growth, national healing and reconciliation, technological advancements, and the upward mobility of our people from poverty into prosperity. These narratives depict a truer picture of Africa than the one told through biased lens.

The Real African Narrative

Africans need to talk about what we have working for us more than what is not. We need to talk more about our progress than we do about the stagnation of yesteryear. Our advancements in healthcare, education, and infrastructure development should take centre stage as they reflect what is taking place in Africa. Instead of focusing on the lack of capital, we need to be proud of the resources that we have. Let us talk more about the gold, diamonds, and the array of precious minerals that we have instead of the fiat currencies we lack, which fluctuate daily and rely on our resources for value and stability. Let us broadcast our tourist attractions rather than the squatter camps that are a temporary feature, as we are busy building more houses for everyone, after all, we have more than enough land to do so. Let us change the way the world has been trying to make us look at ourselves. We are not what anybody wants us to look like; we look like our heavenly Father; we are created in the image of God and we should focus on broadcasting that.

It is our job to tell Africa's true story. Too many sad stories have already been spread even before we were born, but now that we are here and we have all these platforms to like social media at our disposal, let us set the record straight. The dominant perceptions about Africa that we have today are the result of the bad stories that were told before but let us disrupt this old narrative and begin with a positive story. We have a story to tell; so, let us all tell the true African story!

Changing Your Personal Narrative

When God is the source in our lives, we will never run dry. As life would have it, things may become difficult and wthe challenges of life may increase, and like our continent, we might experience a negative flow that results in us losing. However, if we remain connected to God through Christ, rivers of living water will continue to flow out of us, thereby making us more than conquerors regardless of circumstances. The Bible says that *"You shall know the truth and the truth shall set you free"* (John 8: 32). This is a very powerful statement because what you do not know will keep you captive even when you are free. However, once you know that you are connected to an unending flow, you will appreciate that even though weeping may endure through the night, joy comes eventually. Knowledge of the truth is liberating. Our people are groping in the dark yet they are wired for great exploits because they do not know who they are, they are destroyed, weakened, and eventually killed for a lack of knowledge and understanding of who they are. (Hosea 4:6) Once the truth is known and activated, we will crawl out of our misery right to the pinnacle of life knowing that rivers of water are flowing from within us. Our words cease to become mere words; they become transformative words that hold and control destiny. Our lives cease to be a statistic; we become world changers.

Down with Ignorance

The biggest battle we are fighting is that of ignorance. If people are ignorant of God's truth, the devil is happy because he can keep them bound and imprisoned. The purpose of this writing is to encourage each one of us to understand that we are more than animals and we cannot continue in ignorance. Our Christ did not die in vain that we carry on in defeat, sickness, diseases, violence, regression, stagnation, and hatred. Even in the animal kingdom, such behaviours as are found in our societies are not seen. Once our minds are enlightened, the flow of life will transform everything around us.

The word *'flow'* is in the present continuous tense, meaning that once we have caught on to what has already been achieved for us, and once we start responding to the love of God, and we realise the power of that flow, we begin to live purposefully. Just as every flow or current serves a purpose, which is to bless all that is in its path, we too will begin to bless all those we encounter. Once this truth is known, as the rivers of living waters continue gushing from our lives, we become a blessing in the greater scheme. As small and individual tributaries we will begin to find our place in the greater flow of abundance on the African continent.

CHAPTER THREE

ARE YOU AWARE?
DISCERNING THE CHANGE IN FLOW

—⌘—

"My people perish for a lack of knowledge..."
Hosea 4:6

Did You Know?

My work as a minister and as a businessman has taken me to many parts of our beautiful continent. My love for Africa has kept me working tirelessly with other Africans to create a better future for our posterity - those who will inherit this rich spring from us. In my travels, I could not avoid realising the tremendous amounts of wealth that the continent has been blessed with, the natural resources, the amazing and talented people, the clean air, and so much more. I could not help but take note of the not so rosy side of Africa as well; the poverty, the divisions, the crumbling infrastructure, the absence of dignified housing, poor quality social service delivery, illiteracy, unclean water, and poor sanitation for many communities. Africa can be a paradox and an oxymoron in many regards. How can the inhabitants of a continent so rich, wallow in such a delipidated state and yet our wealth is building palaces and kingdoms in the West and the East? After much study, research, ponderin, and conversations with God and my fellow Africans, the light bulb came on. Our eyes have yet to be illuminated enough to bring us to a consciousness of what we are walking on in terms of wealth. We are yet to appreciate how powerful we are as a people. More importantly, we are still ignorant of the billions that are resident in the minds and the talents of our people that are flowing in and out of our continent's villages, towns, and cities annually. And even when we have had our eyes opened to the wealth and limitless possibilities available to us, like the ten spies who disagreed with Joshua and Caleb, we still see ourselves as grasshoppers who are incapable of leveraging the good of the land to our benefit. A lot of our suffering is born out of ignorance.

Facts About Our Flows

Economic Flows

According to the International Monetary Fund, the total production of Africa 54 states in 2019 amounted to US$2,58 trillion. This represents the official annual economic activity registered within Africa for the year. This is just shy of the GDP of France for that same year. If Africa were a singular economy, we would be the 8th largest economy in the world, ahead of Italy and Brazil. This follows years of compounded economic growth in Africa and we are yet to plateau, meaning there is still a lot of growth potential that we are yet to unlock. We have achieved such with limited access to global capital, poor and inadequate infrastructure, a fragmented continental and regional economy, corruption, and the many challenges we are yet to surmount. One can only wonder how productive we will be if we made a few small and yet fundamental and significant changes. While our current economic productivity is insufficient as far as securing the fortunes of our population of 1,3 billion Africans, this can be grown and multiplied over time by making the right approaches and moves.

We are already seeing the fastest growing economies in the world emerging from Africa; the likes of Rwanda, Senegal, and Ethiopia topping the list and registering annual growth rates upwards 7%. If this can be sustained and expanded into other nations, we will see the continent leap forward and empower itself to solve its complexities.

Agricultural Potential

Furthermore, the Africa Development Bank reports that Africa's agricultural sector is set to become a US$1 trillion industry by 2030. With 65% of the world's arable stock of land, Africa is in a favourable position to feed itself and have a surplus to feed other continents too. Africa's agricultural sector carries breath-taking growth potential, we simply need to marry our agriculture with financial investment, technology, and entrepreneurship to accelerate the growth of this sector and realise its potential. In so doing we will be able to drive a mega industrialisation of the agro-sector and create jobs in research and development, manufacturing, financial and capital markets, logistics, infrastructure, and export.

Human Capital

As far as the future of human capital is concerned Africa is the future. With a median age of 19,7 years and a population of 1,3 billion. Africa represents the future of the world. It is predicted that by 2030 Africa's youth will constitute 42% of the global youth population. Our youthful population represents a golden opportunity for accelerated growth and innovation on the continent. This is happening at a time when more advanced economies will be faced with an increasingly ageing population, which will saddle them with the high costs of elderly health care and there will also be a huge demand for skilled labour, which the African will be able to pump. This was the case in the 1400s, when the developed world looked to Africa for quality human capital to staff their industries. The difference this time will be that we are not going to migrate as slaves or cheap labour but as high-level thinkers within global thinktanks, CEO's of Fortune 500 companies, investors on the world's key bourses, and professors in the Ivy League institutions of higher learning.

Mineral Wealth

Our continent is rich beyond our wildest imagination. We host over 30% of the world's known mineral reserves. This excludes the undiscovered minerals. The Democratic Republic of Congo alone is said to be the richest country in the world in terms of natural resources, and God chose to locate that piece of earth on the Great Continent. Its known deposits were estimated to be worth over US$24 trillion at current prices (2019). Globally Africa accounts for the bulk of diamond, platinum, and gold production. No continent can boast to enjoy the same degree of wealth per capita and per square kilometre like Africa can.

Energy Potential

Africa is on the verge of an energy boom in both fossil fuels and renewable energy. Five of the top thirty oil-producing nations are in Africa. Proven oil reserves had grown by more than 150 per cent, increasing from 53.4 billion barrels since 1980, to 130.3 billion barrels by the end of 2012. And they are set to grow even more with discoveries continually being sighted in different parts of Africa. Investment into the oil and gas sector alone is expected to rise to over US$2 trillion by 2036.

Blessed with incredible weather and an abundant network of rivers and dams Africa is also on the verge of a clean energy revolution. According to the International Renewable Energy Agency, by 2030 Africa will derive up to 22% of its total final energy consumption from renewable energy sources, a fourfold increase from 5% in 2013. This means that Africa will be a vibrant and continually industrialising continent with a much lower carbon footprint than what you find in the developed world. We are emerging at the perfect time when innovations allow us to enjoy the benefits of low-cost power generation without destroying the environment. Africa can easily choose to the home of clean and environmentally friendly cities.

Diaspora Remittances

The World Bank reports that remittances into Africa from its diaspora amounted to about US$48 billion in 2019 alone. This means that the African Diaspora is sending home money that is almost equivalent to the annual production of Tanzania, Africa's tenth-largest economy. This makes the African Diaspora an economy by itself that needs to be organised and further empowered to excel. We need to recruit the African Diaspora as a crucial partner in development and offer them a seat at the dinner table. They possess the economic resources, skills, expertise, and exposure that can prove valuable to Africa's leap into the future.

With African continuing to migrate into the Diaspora and providing much needed critical skills there, this represents a huge flow that needs to be harnessed and channelled appropriately away from just expenditures and into investment as well. Imagine if we developed partnerships between entrepreneurs in Africa and African financiers in the Diaspora. We can create opportunities by unlocking the value chain in an amazing way.

Market Depth

According to the Brookings Institution, Africa is one of the fastest-growing consumer markets in the world. Household consumption continues to increase even faster than its gross domestic product (GDP) in recent years—and that average annual GDP growth has consistently outpaced the global average. Africa's affluence is on the rise, her population is growing, urbanisation rates are on the incline, and access to the internet is growing rapidly and mobile phones on the continent are now ubiquitous, Africa's emerging economies are whetting the appetites of many investors as it presents exciting opportunities for expansion in retail and distribution.

In fact, consumer expenditure on the continent has grown at a compound annual rate of 3.9 percent since 2010 and reached $1.4 trillion in 2015. This figure is expected to reach $2.1 trillion by 2025, and $2.5 trillion by 2030. If the Continental Free Trade Area (CFTA) is properly implemented, by 2030 a single continental market for goods and services will be operational, offering corporations different points of entry to the continent and a potential market of 1.7 billion people.

Illicit Flows

According to The Brookings Institution in a March 2020 article, between 1980 -2018, Africa exported over US$1,3 trillion in illicit flows through illegal activities like under-pricing of resources and exports, tax evasion, corruption, and smuggling. Imagine the schools, hospitals, infrastructure, and investments that could have been made if all this money had been retained locally and utilised within the continental economy. Can you see the difference these flows would have had on livelihoods and the ease of doing business within our nations had we been more diligent about managing our flows?

Africa's Kairos

> *So, Philip ran to him, and heard him*
> *reading the prophet Isaiah, and said, "Do you understand*
> *what you are reading?"*
> **Acts 8:30**

When we look at the facts above, which are just a microcosm and a tip of the iceberg of what is flowing through our continent. Do we truly appreciate the meaning and possible impact of these facts? Do we as Africans see that the tide is turning in our favour? Are we conscious of the fact that our decade of emergence is upon us? It is time we wake up and smell the coffee and remove the lenses that have been tainting our view and perspective of ourselves, our continent, and our times. We need to adopt a new prophetic paradigm and worldview. One that empowers us to discern the times and the shifting flow in time so we can effectively reorient, restructure, and reposition ourselves as individuals, families, communities, entrepreneurs, industry, churches, and governments. We need to do this with a sense of urgency.

What I spelt out about the emerging flows represents potential and opportunity. All these truths and realities will not benefit us much unless we start working together so that collectively we can turn this rising tide in our favour. A lot of work awaits us, my brothers and sisters. We are the stewards of this spring and all its flows. We are expected to be found faithful in this regard. For to whom much is given, much is also required. (Luke 12:48)

Knowing How to Respond

"of the sons of Issachar who had understanding of the times, to know what Israel ought to do, their chiefs were two hundred; and all their brethren were at their command;"

1 Chronicles 12:32

The tribe of Issachar was known for its knack for discerning times and seasons and aligning their activities appropriately. They were a prophetic company who always knew what Israel ought to be focusing its energies on in any epoch or period. How we desperately need such men and women on the continent today. They are a critical resource to have in these times. We need them in industry, trade, commerce, culture, arts, media, the church, government, education, and healthcare. Discerning leaders are needed at all levels of from the village to the state, regional, and continental levels. Our churches must raise and release such people into all our political, economic, and social structures, lest we continue to be a case of the blind leading the blind and falling into the ditch of despondency. (Matthew 15:14)

These men and women are the Joseph's of our times who are capable of strategically positioning our continent for the rising tide. Joseph as you may recall, was able to co-ordinate the Egyptian economy by managing the flows of the harvests of the land. In the seven years of plenty, he reserved twenty per cent of the nation's agricultural output in a strategic reserve. In the seven years of famine, he unlocked the storehouses, and the land of Egypt began to flow with plenty and abundance when the world had lack and famine. Joseph had perceived that the magnanimous flow that would hit Egypt in the seven years of plenty, would one day prove extremely valuable in the seven years of famine that people would trade their entire wealth to access a small part of the flow he would have preserved.

This saw the flow changing significantly as many nations came with their wealth to buy grain from Egypt. Even when the currency failed, they exchanged their cattle for grain and Egypt became considerably wealthy in a time of crisis. He positioned the nation for the shifting flow because of the prophetic insight he had. Joseph discerned the shifting flow ahead of time and positioned the nation to prosper because of the changing tide. He was able to not only interpret the complex dreams of Pharaoh but was able to devise a plan of action that would ensure that the tide would turn in their favour.

Africa Unite

And the LORD said, "Indeed the people are one and they all have one language, and this is what they begin to do; now nothing that they propose to do will be withheld from them.

Genesis 11:6

I like the concept of unity because it restores our lost pride. When the colonisers took over the continent, they employed a very shrewd and effective system of divide and rule that Africa is still grappling to break loose from. This system made the process of plunder much easier for them to effect. Therefore, to change of flow of money, power, and resources we must unite as brothers and sisters. It is only by working and doing things together that we will prosper and live victoriously.

As diverse as we are, we need to find agreement on key issues that have the power to turn the tables in our favour. Now more than ever we must cut covenants at continental, regional, national, provincial and community levels where we agree to put the interests of Africa ahead of our individual interests. We need governments, business, civic players, churches, and the citizens of Africa to agree that that time to restructure Africa is now.

Our agreements should look at how we can further bolster our free trade area which comes on board in 2021. We should look at collaborating in building our infrastructure, in pooling financial resources together, in building regional innovation hubs, and regional power pools for electricity, and we can start negotiating with multilateral institutions as a continent, among others. Unity is the song we must sing going forward and our God will bless us. When we unite as speak as one, nothing shall be impossible for us.

A Few Ideas

We can achieve this repositioning and restructuring by making a few simple yet effective moves. These moves do not require multilateral financing from the Bretton Woods institutions or the BRICS development bank. They only need inclusive engagement and agreement on our part, and we will see the sleeping giant called Africa emerge and assert herself as the global force she was created to be.

1. Adopting Community Empowerment Approaches to Investment

A much-needed shift is required in our approach to empowering communities. We need to put the communities at the centre of the benefit system of each investment on our continent, regardless of how large or micro it might be. This kind of system can be implemented at all levels. For example, if a school is to be constructed in a village, the company should use the labour from the villages in the vicinity, and the building materials must be sourced from the local area. We should use these developments to support African innovators such as Technology for Tomorrow, which produces low cost resilient bricks in Uganda. The local hardware shops must supply locally produced cement, paint, roofing materials and everything else that is required. At the end of the construction, there must be an economy that can still run itself and with the potential to grow. Women in the area can be empowered to start a bakery to supply bread for both the school community and the villagers. The school can also be empowered to run its growers' scheme for local farmers to supply it with meat and vegetables for the students.

2. A New Paradigm for Shrinking Industries

The mining sector is finite. Its resources are non-renewable. Once extracted and exported the minerals are gone for good. This means as Africa we must find ways of maximising the value and the benefit we derive from the mineral sector while the extracts are still on African soil. Historically, mining operations have left our communities with nothing to show for all that economic activity and the billions extracted except for environmental hazards. If we are to maximise the flows of mineral wealth in the favour of our communities and nations, we need to change how investment in this industry works. Firstly, most of our mines are found in underdeveloped areas meaning there is an infrastructure deficit. Secondly, there is little economic activity in those areas. To address these deficiencies mining project must contribute to infrastructural development efforts, community share ownership schemes, and local economic development initiatives that will stimulate a sustainable economy in that community. This will allow for an economy to continue long after the resources have been depleted.

Here are a few illustrations, if a mining project starts somewhere, all the materials for building staff housing must be provided by the locals. If a mine hospital is to be developed, all the materials must be supplied by the local businesspeople who must employ locals only. Only when there are no local experts should we draw on skills from outside the local community. Once the mine is operational, the processing and refining of the mineral ore must be done locally, and if possible, only the final product can then be exported. A step further must be explored where factories that require that kind of mineral can be set up close to the mine and grow the cities and industries around the mining community. This is the change of flow that Africa needs and must be known for as the world supplier. A simple example is our iron and steel industry. With growing global demand for iron and steel we should not be exporting ore but refined steel to the end-user nations. This change of flow will strengthen local economies and will bring confidence to the local people as they realise that they can do their own things successfully without some outside intervention

3. A New Approach to Energy

Africa's energy potential is massive. If we began to build refineries and industries within our oil-producing regions, we stand to unlock a tremendous value chain that will create jobs for our youth and boundless opportunities for our entrepreneurs. One only needs to look at the United Arab Emirates for a glimpse of what certain parts of Africa could potentially evolve into if this sector were managed with greater intentionality. Again, we must come together and build the infrastructure that will allow us to interconnect regionally and internally. We need to build transnational consortiums to this end and build our own domestic and intercontinental oil pipelines. This will help us to lower the cost of fuel, significantly reduce our cost of doing business and our energy import bill. This will also effectively improve our competitiveness in global markets across various industries.

Electricity is another area that we can unlock a great and massive flow in. According to a 2011 IPCC report, Africa is said to have only tapped into 5% of its hydropower generation capacity. A massive energy revolution is taking place on the continent as we speak. The Grand Inga Dam project in the Democratic Republic of the Congo and the Great Renaissance Dam in Ethiopia are amazing cases in point. These show that Africa is set to electrify its industries and rural spaces and lower its cost of doing business dramatically over time. This will open opportunities to unlock an even greater economic flow, but we must be discerning.

4. Domestic and Diasporan Partnerships

Africa has a very talented, skilled, and experienced Diaspora. We have seen sons of our soil who have since relocated into more developed economies rise financially, entrepreneurially, and professionally. Some have risen to manage and control huge investment portfolios, of which if we were built smart alliances, we can experience an entrepreneurship boom by marrying the ideas of continentally resident Africans and the skills, influence, exposure, and financial capacity of the Diasporan Africans. Influential Africans in the Diaspora like Special Envoy of the Africa Union Strive Masiyiwa has used his influence and muscle as a Diasporan, to create the Africa Medical Supply platform, which seeks to reduce the corruption element within the procurement of vital medical supplies to African countries. His intervention allows public healthcare institutions to access supplies at affordable prices and improves the access for the most vulnerable. Imagine if we can do this on various levels of the influence chain, we can unlock so much in this regard and see a greater flow emerge from Africa to the world.

Time for Courageous Joshua's to Rise

Africa has proven that we have the vision, skills, capabilities, and the goodwill necessary for us to leap forward into our illustrious future. What remains is to marry all these positives with courage. I derive a lot of courage and deep insights from a great leader in the Bible called Joshua. He is one inspiring leader who empowered his people because he knew how to change the flow. In the book of Joshua chapter 10, we read from verse 5 as follows:

"Then the five kings of the Amorites, the kings of Jerusalem, Hebron, Jarmuth, Lachish and Eglon joined forces. They moved up with all their troops and took up positions against Gibeon and attacked it. The Gibeonites then sent a word to Joshua in the camp

at Gilgal: "Do not abandon your servants, come up to us quickly and save us! Help us, because all the Amorite kings from the hill country have joined forces against us."

Now the above scripture paints a very scary picture. Two things Joshua could have done: tell the Gibeonites to go and defend themselves or surrender to the five nations as slaves. Courageous leaders never do the easy thing; they operate with a level of discernment that is not common. They always do the right thing even when it is scary. Joshua inquired of the Lord in prayer and God answered him and said, *"Go and pursue them and none will escape from you."*

He clearly understood the response from God and was very careful not to miss what God had instructed him, as you will see shortly. The normal flow was to surrender because they were outnumbered, but after consulting God, Joshua was given the go-ahead to change the FLOW. Please understand – this is critical. In this world, it is going to be rough and tough, but with the Creator of Heaven and Earth, the Father of our Saviour and Lord Jesus Christ, we can change the flow. Even if we are in the minority we are advantaged because with God we are always victorious. We have already gone from being slaves to placing a man of African descent in the Oval Office. We have gone from being cheap labour on our continent to building the largest businesses on the continent. History is flowered with what we can achieve and attain when we choose the audacity of courage over the sensibility of fear. To a discerning leader, the odds may be stacked against them, but they always possess the bravado necessary to lead their people to conquest.

Courage in Action

Verse 8 of the same chapter says, *"And the Lord said unto Joshua, fear them not; for I have delivered them into thine hand; there shall not a man of them stand before thee."* Here is a typical example of how God changed the flow of things for Joshua. All odds were against him, but God, knowing the reality on the ground, which was a bloody reality for Joshua and his people, still said to him, 1) fear not, 2) I have given them all to you, and 3) none of them shall escape. God gave Joshua a single command and two promises, that was enough to bring Joshua's courage to the fore.

The first thing that happens to anybody when confronted with something bigger than them that one was not prepared for is fear, and Joshua is no exception. We all know that the number one characteristic of fear is that it paralyses even the most competent among us. In that state, we cannot function, so God said, *"I will reverse the normal; do not fear."* When faced with adversity, fear is supposed to be dominant, but God removes that fear and replaces it with courage and boldness. The natural environment will have no option but to respond in your favour. That is how the flow changes. It begins with turning fear into courage.

The second point was that he was God told him, *"I have not only surrounded them, but I have given them to you".* In other words, Joshua was being told that his job has been cut out for him; the enemies will try to do what they know, but if he follows the strategy, they will be confused by the response and become paralysed, thereby confirming the power of the change of flow. Joshua knew these armies would try to flex their muscles, but his invisible Heavenly support system was now operational; therefore, he had no need to stress. Joshua triggered the change in the flow of the battle the moment he told his armies to rise and pursue the enemy and everything changed.

The third point was that none of them would escape. This was another very critical point for Joshua to follow because when God has spoken, every word is life and has meaning. Every one of them needed to be killed. If not, they will raise a seed that will be toxic to the entire world. So, Joshua had to address the sun and the moon to stop and give him enough daylight time to finish these people. The two elements had no choice but to stop until the assignment was fulfilled.

Change in Flow

The change of flow is a great concept that is applied in many applications but called by different names. In football, managers instruct their players to be closely observant of their opponents, especially at the onset of every match. If the opponents start with a fast-paced game and that is the other team's strength, the opposing team will be beaten when they do not have the stamina for that kind of game. So, clever managers are quick to observe that, and they can counter their opponent by slowing down the game to suit their style of play, thereby applying the change of flow.

Transformation is inevitable once the change of flow is applied. The small nation which was overwhelmingly outnumbered by five strong nations stood their ground and that changed the flow. They saw five nations fleeing before them and they destroyed every man and their kings.

Turnaround is Now

"...now I will show this people favour"
Exodus 3:21

2010 was a milestone year for Africa. For the first time in the history of football, the World Cup was hosted in Africa by an African nation. This was a grand opportunity that allowed us to showcase our ability to deliver an exceptional tournament that met global standards. This was a turning point in our fortunes. One that allowed us to broadcast our virtue to the world. Interestingly, the punch line for this tournament was a Tswana word, *"ke nako,"* which means *"It is our time."* We may not have seen the prophetic nature of the event and the punchline, but the truth be told, Africa had just entered its own. Indeed, our time is now.

Whenever I think of Africa's time, I am reminded of the time when Israel was under Egyptian bondage. They toiled and laboured for 430 years and they had nothing to show for it. The Scriptures say that Pharaoh set taskmasters over them. These, he assigned as slave drivers whose mandate was to extract the most out the blood, sweat, and tears of the Israelites. They were used to build store cities for Pharaoh. He worked them like beasts of burden to the point where their labour was so hard, they turned to the God of their forefathers for deliverance. It was then that God remembered His covenant and promise to Abraham. The Lord had promised Abraham that his descendants would be in captivity 400 years, but after which they would be liberated and with that, they would come out with great substance.

It is amazing how when the time for God to turn their captivity around, it was sudden and so amazing they felt as though they were dreaming. God promised to show them favour. With it a significant transfer of wealth from the hands of the slave masters into theirs. I believe that Africa is at a similar defining point in her destiny. We are about to experience a turnaround that has yet to be imagined. Many Africans both young and old, are becoming more and more audacious in their entrepreneurial pursuits regardless of scale or industry. Take Nigeria as an example, we are seeing more and more bankers of African descent taking up a greater market share of Africa's most populous nation and largest economy. We have seen the likes of Strive Masiyiwa, the mobile telephony magnate, rising to dominate the telecoms sector in many African nations and penetrate territories beyond Africa such as New Zealand, and the United Kingdom. Such strides are accelerating our turnaround and improving the position of Africa in capturing the flow to our benefit and the betterment of the livelihoods of our people.

Africa is now in her time and season. We need to know what we ought to do so we can operate in sync with the times and seasons that the Father has set. When we function in harmony with the calendar of the Spirit we walk in prosperity and blessing, as we can only bear fruit in season if we properly align ourselves with the tide. This means we need new policy frameworks. We need new incentives and initiatives that will inspire and encourage more of our people to take risks and pursue their boldest and wildest dreams. Instead of posturing ourselves as a hopeless case for dead aid, we need to focus on unlocking value, attracting investment, and creating new trade networks so that when the tide rises, we can channel the flow effectively and accordingly. We need to focus on bringing more and more of our marginalised brothers and sisters into the mainstream economy and connecting them to prime markets for their goods and services.

It is our time for a turnaround, and we must restructure, realign, and reform our governments, economies, and societies to this end. Warring and conflicting tribes, political parties, and nations must now dialogue and resolve the deep-seated contentious issues that have kept them divided for centuries. We need to effect improved transitional mechanisms that allow power to be transferred as seamlessly as possible so that investment and human capital feel safe within our borders. It is indeed our time, and it is time we start function accordingly.

In life generally, the areas that have caused untold pain are areas where there has been stagnation. Governments come and go; hence, the process of democracy. Anywhere major problems are found, some leaders refused to hand over power peacefully and seamlessly. The toxic politics behind this power retention attitudes are a result of selfish people. They want things only for themselves and do not think about others; in other words, they did not want to change the flow of things in the new way of governance.

The Coincidence Course

A study of the Hebrew language and culture will show that there is no word for coincidence. This is because the concept of coincidence, happenstance, or fate does not exist in their context. A coincidence suggests that at least two independent paths came into contact and connection without conscious human effort. To the Hebrew mind whenever two unrelated and uncoordinated events or acts link, it is perceived as an act of God. This is what is happening on the continent, a lot of key and crucial pieces are coming into their right place and at the right time. This is the African reality. We are coming into our own at the perfect time. It is our responsibility to pay attention to the flows and their patterns. As we do, we will become more discerning as the changes begin to happen. The following story will illustrate what I mean.

Follow the Flow

I like to tell a story about one of the testimonies in my book called, *"The Spirit of a Champion."* A man was following one of our advertising trucks, which he had admired for a very long time and felt that he needed to talk to the owner of the vehicle. It took a couple of days because he was walking and tracking where the truck came from and where it was going. Finally, he arrived at the gate of our premises. As the security guard was opening the gate, he was amazed to see a crazy-looking man with stinking, greasy clothes and long, dusty hair. He called him a mad man. This man forced his way through until he arrived at the reception. He was left there alone because the whole admin staff and receptionist had fled the area. They had never seen this kind of mad man at the office; people who looked like this are found walking along the highway and they ate from dustbins. Eventually, someone came knocking at my door to warn me to be very careful because we had been (invaded) by a crazy man. I took courage and walked towards the reception area, and it was true that we had been invaded. The man looked scary, but I had to be strong for everyone. A few minutes later I was in the boardroom chatting to my new friend who was telling me a long and very sad story of the events of his life. By the grace of God, I saw the value in this brother and beyond what had brought him to this stage of life. Together with my team, we helped him to look good, to clean him up, and to write down his vision again; that became the beginning of a transformed life. The value that was given to him revived his passion for life and today, he is a group managing director of an international company. Every human being on the face of the earth was qualified by God to be here and has great value, which the enemy of our souls desperately wants to crush and frustrate.

Here is how the flow changed. Everyone who saw this man in his former state called him names, and rightfully so, judging by the standards of this world. I could have called the police as I was being advised, and the security authorities could have arrested this man for trespassing. I chose to change the normal flow of things and to see value in that brother. Today, he has added so much value in other people's lives who, in turn, are doing the same to others.

CHAPTER FOUR

SHIFTING THE FLOW OF IDEAS, WEALTH & POWER

—∞—

"Every generation must out of relative obscurity, discover its mission, fulfil it or betray"
Franz Fanon

Power to the People

Every generation is called to make its own set of sacrifices for the advancement of future generations. I believe that my generation has a lot of work to do in preparing a better landscape for future generations of Africans to excel and rise to the peak of their potential. We must reconfigure and level the playing field so that the continent can enter her time and season ready to maximise the opportunities that Africa can harness. We must also prepare, mentor, and coach the next generation for exploits. We are to invest in them the skills, sensitivities, and systems that they need to excel when their season to take the reins comes.

To change the direction of the flow in Africa's favour, we must redirect the flow of ideas, wealth, and power so that our people experience real empowerment. This redirection will lead greater capacity to tap into the magnanimous flow within our continent. Ideas represent the fruit of our minds - our skills, labour, technology, knowledge, intellectual properties, innovations, creativity, and entrepreneurship. Wealth speaks of our factors of production and our productive sectors - mineral resources, our markets, opportunities, industries, and land. Power speaks to our political processes and policy frameworks; our state institutions and how our states are structured, led and governed. These three flows are at the centre of our growth economically and institutionally. How we manage these fundamental flows will determine how much more we can unlock to the benefit of our people and continent.

Our Generational Legacy

The historical backdrop depicts a continent were none of these flows favoured Africa and Africans. Our best flows were systematically captured by colonial and imperial powers and all flowed westward and that without a doubt had to change. In the 15th century, Africa lost some of its most agile and able young talent to the slave trade, the 19th and 20th centuries saw our wealth and power being drained from the continent through colonialism and imperialism. The realisation that we had been reduced to second class citizens on our own soil inspired a generation of many young men and women to make tremendous sacrifices to change this unacceptable status quo. These brave and courageous youths are celebrated today as the founding fathers of Africa; Kwame Nkrumah, Julius Nyerere, Jomo Kenyatta, Nelson Mandela, Kenneth Kaunda, Haile Selassie, Thomas Sankara, and Robert Mugabe among many others. These icons were able to change the direction of the flow of political power within our nations by fighting for democracies to be born across the entirety of Africa. Such bold decisions are never easy to reach because the consequences of such courageous acts are always dire, in the case of our liberators' generation, many lives were lost, but the flow and balance of power needed to change and as such the requisite price had to be paid. They paid the price and as a result we are now a free and liberated continent.

How They Did It

These men and women led so inspiringly that we saw a pulling together of Africans within respective nations across tribal, generational, economic, educational and even ideological lines to change the flow. Eventually, alliances were formed across borders, which saw the formation of the Organisation of Africa Unity in Addis Ababa in 1963, with a clear mandate of ensuring that the entire continent would be liberated from all forms of oppression. No sacrifice was considered too great for this cause. The result of this was the successful dislodging of colonial powers and the establishment of a new order; an order where the flow of power was finally in the hands of the majority. Now the true shareholders and owners of Africa could determine their future and destiny through the exercise of their democratic right through the ballot.

The Curse of An Incomplete Change of Flow

As we progressed in our newfound political liberation, we soon realised that defeating colonialism in the political space represented the genesis of a shift in Africa's flows. It was a beginning and not an end. More and more Africans began to develop self-confidence and the desire to have a say in determining their destinies, so they began to explore various opportunities in industry and commerce. New businesses were birthed by young African entrepreneurs, and innovative ideas were conceptualised as many were ready to enjoy the fruit of our freedom and our Promised Land. It would not be long before there was a realisation once again that the new normal was found wanting when weighed against the promises of freedom and self-determination. Many Africans are still battling the same economic inequalities that were prevalent before the flow of power had been shifted. We still struggled for access to opportunity. The two other major flows remained channelled and directed towards the development and enrichment of Western economies because of the firm grip their multinationals had on the continental economy.

Decades of battling oppression, emotional, and mental erosion, had taken their toll on our liberators and fatigue set in. We, the citizens had also become complacent and complicit. Our eyes had lost sight of the broader objective of delivering a more prosperous continent for all who are its inhabitants. We found ourselves comfortable with what should have never made us comfortable - an incomplete revolution that failed to shift these three major flows entirely. Fast forward into our contemporary Africa, the movement of ideas and wealth within the continent are still not working in our favour. Our natural resources, innovations, and labour are still not benefiting our people as they should. Our leaders have betrayed the African cause by illegally siphoning money made from Africa in safe havens outside the African continent; a practice that has seen billions leave our shores and serve as low-cost capital, which foreign corporations and economies use to accelerate their growth and prosperity. This is money which would have gone a long way in fuelling ideas and improving the spread of wealth within Africa but here we are, our economies continue to wither and shrivel and we continue to access capital at high and unsustainable interest rates with stringent measures that do nothing but choke our development prospects. The African people and their destinies have been betrayed.

The African Rebellion

There is a new generation of Africans that is emerging on and off the continent. These Africans are endowed with renewed vigour to speak out and regain control of their future. Guided by a new paradigm of thought, this new breed is emerging with the determination and resolve to transform Africa's destiny by changing the flow of ideas, wealth, and power to favour the continent and her 1,3 billion people. Their ideology constitutes a rebellion against the present situation, it is one that believes that we can only effectively change the flow of wealth, ideas, and power by taking ownership of what is ours and developing our continent ourselves. It is a rebellion against the old norm where wealth is concentrated in the hands of a few while the continent is bled continually by a network of nefarious individuals at the expense of the majority.

This new African ideology is centred around how we can change these flows. To change them, we do not need to take up arms and dislodge governments. We just simply need to redesign and reconfigure how we do business with the world and among ourselves in ways that empower us to leverage these flows to create more empowering opportunities, spread the wealth more equitably, and improve our democracies and systems of governance.

Changing the Flow of Ideas

Ideas carry significant economic value. Every business began as an idea. Ideas represent the technical know-how, the abilities, innovations, inventions, strategies, wisdom, knowledge and economic capacities of our people. Ideas are capital in their own way. If you go to Silicon Valley today in search of venture capital or financing from angel investors, they assess the quality of your ideas and their viability. This is because they know the economic value of an idea whose time has come.

For very long the ideas that have built Africa have never really been from Africa. A lot of the developments we have enjoyed in the African economy were colonial and was targeted towards serving the interests of a minority. This allowed minority groups to have an advantage over the majority in this space. They had access to better learning institutions that gave them more exposure than was given to the majority. When freedom and independence came, a chunk of those who had benefited from the old order fled to the West with their reservoirs of knowledge and ideas. Those who remained were not as keen on transferring their knowledge and skills to the betterment of the entire continent and over time, they too left for distant shores. This was then followed by the brain drain which saw African talent leak into the West in search of better opportunities. Since then we have lost most of our ideas to the already developed West and most recently the East through brain drain, indigenous intellectual property, and entrepreneurial potential.

For as long as we do not begin to reform our economies so that the talent we develop is inspired and motivated to stay on the continent and pursue their greatest dreams here, we will continue to lose our investment in them. Our young engineers, medical experts, mathematicians, technological whizz kids, and entrepreneurs will continue to leave the continent for greener pastures in distant shores. This sees us losing a lot of our quality thinkers and technocrats, those with the know-how and abilities we so desperately need to shift the flow in our favour.

Educational Reform

"As a man thinks..."

Proverbs 23:7

To achieve this long-overdue change in the flow of ideas, we need to transform the thinking of our people. The best way to ensure a broad-based transformation is, to begin with, our education systems as they have a reach that is both deep and wide. While we do not have as many schools as we need, we have schools even in the most remote of areas. This represents an asset we need to maximise to our growth and transformation. Most of our educational frameworks were inherited from colonial powers and were only slightly realigned and expanded to reach most of our people. Something we are grateful to our liberators for. However, the models and thinking that guided these institutions is now ancient and archaic and will not suffice to change the flow of ideas in this hyperconnected global village. We need to up our game and reform our systems of education.

There are certain subjects in our educational systems that are completely irrelevant to our needs and our future. Those must be removed and replaced with subjects relevant to the fourth industrial revolution and Africa's strengths. Our people must be equipped with the skills and competencies that help us build our local industries and economies at every level. Why should children study Western world history when they do not know their African history? Why don't we focus on the in-depth study of our minerals and their uses so that we turn our students into creative masters of their destinies? We should invest more into agricultural tuition at both primary and secondary levels of education and teach our children that agriculture is a viable business with the potential to revolutionise their fortunes. We need to reform the education sector to move our children beyond mastering basic literacies and make them competent drivers and catalysts to the industrialisation of Africa. Our schools and institutions must teach entrepreneurship, science, technology, engineering, mathematics, the arts, and the many other skills that our economies need to become globally competitive.

As the flow of thinking changes, the focus must be Africa. I am not saying we should forget the outside world, but we need to be extensively educated about our continent more than we currently are. We need to educate future generations on a vision of a prosperous Africa. We need to culture them to lead and be pioneers, initiators, innovators, inventors, problem solvers and solution providers who will bring this vision to reality.

Embracing Technology as A Game Changer

Technology has been coined the game changer of our times. Information Communications Technology is the infrastructure of the present and future global economy. Technology has accelerated our ability to bridge the development divide and leap our continent forward by several years. For example, our rural areas which were in the past referred to as remote areas, are not as remote anymore. Through advancements in fibre optics, clean energy, mobile and satellite technology, even our rural communities are connected to the world through the internet. This presents us with a golden opportunity to bridge the chasm between rural and urban schools so we can give rural students access and exposure to quality tuition equal to that being offered in a top tier private school in suburban Africa.

Embracing technology in the reform of our educational sector is a no brainer, which will open a plethora of opportunities that we need to leverage and harness to change the flow of ideas. This allows us the broaden the reach of quality education and remove barriers that impede most of our rural talent from gaining access to life-transforming opportunities and competences. My God, I can see that army of well-educated young African men and women, drawn from both rural and urban schools, armed, not with machetes and AK47's, but with the skills, literacies, competencies, and the expertise to change the flow

Changing the Flow of Wealth

To change the flow of wealth, we must start with a few simple changes in how we do business. These changes do not even require much effort to implement, just the political will. For so long the absence of political will has impeded the potential and progress of Africa's entrepreneurs and our indigenous workforce. Initiating them will have a tremendous downstream effect that will finally see the African Spring benefiting the African people in real and tangible ways. Simple examples include ensuring that all monies generated locally are deposited and invested within our local financial institutions so they can support our local industries and create entrepreneurial opportunities and jobs for our people. Identifying companies in the world that need what we have and inviting them to establish their companies on our continent in win/win partnerships with our locals is another approach to shifting the flow of wealth. A good example of this is how the government of Botswana created Debswana, a joint venture company between the Botswana government and DeBeers. Through Debswana, Botswana has been able to drive development, lift more of its people out of poverty, improve access to basic social services and amenities, achieve budget surpluses and create jobs and opportunities.

The Clean Energy Revolution

Africa is blessed with an abundance of renewable energy

sources. As we all know green energy is the future. Seeing that we are poised for this huge industrialisation program, the continent is divinely set for success because the hydroelectric potential that can be unlocked in the Great Lakes region of Africa is breath-taking. The abundantly shining African sun also signals more clean energy sources which if harnessed the entire continent will be able to do business at a much lower the unit cost while creating avenues for a more inclusive economy. This will make us less dependent on the world for our energy needs and more importantly, it will fuel our domestic economic growth and ensure more wealth can be placed in the hands of the African people. With electric cars representing the future of mobility, we can become less reliant on the Middle East for traditional oil-based fuels, thus minimising the flows that exit our continent unnecessarily.

Stimulating Domestic Entrepreneurship Through Downstream Industries

Most of the investment strategies of the past were very wrong and should not be allowed to perpetuate. Investors were coming into the African economies to extract natural resources and no beneficiation of those resources was enforced. What was left at the end of the day, were desolate communities and ghost towns with large mining dumps and acid water everywhere. Think about this process: our young men and women who had worked all their lives in these abandoned mines are now left to die; jobless, without an income, and infected by all kinds of sicknesses from working in these hazardous environments. The investors took their profits to banks domiciled in their home nations, for further investments towards their development agenda and yet nothing was left to show for the extracted minerals back in Africa. These were win/lose arrangements as they won entirely, and we lost entirely.

The same goes for our farming industry; huge tracts of land are used to produce tobacco and huge auctions have been set up to sell the tobacco leaves to overseas processors. Globally, tobacco is a trillion-dollar industry by annual sales. Can you imagine if a third of the world's cigarettes were being produced on the continent? The flow of money would take a new and dramatic turn. If an investor is keen to invest on the continent, they must use local industries to produce all materials, if resources are not locally available, we should look for them from another African state before we even consider sources beyond the continent. All the required developments must engage local skills, beginning with the communities where the investments are located, and more importantly, profits must be returned to the continent and reinvested in those communities first.

It must also become mandatory that no raw materials should leave the continent without beneficiation. We should focus on building downstream industries around our resources like processing and assembly plants to turn our natural resources into more valuable finished goods.

Spreading the Wealth

Africa needs new economic systems if we are to effectively spread the wealth to all levels. For example, if an agricultural estate is to be set up in a community, a local company should be given such a contract, labour, and the building materials must be sourced from the villages in the vicinity. The local hardware shops must supply locally produced cement, irrigation equipment, paint, roofing materials and everything else that is required. A grower's scheme must be set up by the estate company, to ensure that locals are contributing to the development of that industry as well. Where possible, locals should be empowered to add value to the produce and form a part of the supply chain within the national, regional and international markets. As the estate is developing, we must have unlocked the value chain so the local economy can also run itself with the potential to grow. Women in the area can be encouraged to start bakeries, poultry, and gardening projects to supply the school daily with enough supply for the community.

We can do the same with the mining industry. If a mining project starts somewhere, all the materials for building staff housing must be provided by the locals. These local businesses must be required to employ locals only unless there are no local experts available. Once the mine is operational, the processing of the minerals must be done locally and if possible, only the final product can then be exported. A further step must be explored where factories that require that kind of mined products can be set up close to the mine, so we can grow cities and industries around the mining community.

This is the change of flow that Africa needs and must be known for as the world supplier. This change of flow will strengthen local economies by putting money into the hands of locals. This concept will jump-start the local economy and we need to be strategic about ensuring the sustainable development of these local economies. This will also bring confidence to our local people as they realise that they can build and run their own enterprises successfully without some outside interference.

Changing the Flow of Power

"The thing you are doing is not good. Thou wilt surely wear away, both thou, and this people that is with thee: for this thing is too heavy for thee; thou art not able to perform it thyself alone."

Exodus 18: 17,18

From the book of Exodus 18: 17–18, we derive deep wisdom that changed the lives of the people of God as they journeyed to their land of promise. The wisdom is that when power is concentrated among a few individuals and institutions, it becomes destructive and as we have seen in history, it corrupts. Consider how after political independence came to Africa, most of the liberation organisations who had to transform into governments struggled with the concept of democracy because they had a sense of entitlement. As such they were not too keen on sharing power with those who were not freedom fighters, leaving many technocrats, thinkers, and astute minds barred from the corridors of power and treated with undue suspicion. This concentration of political power in the liberator's hands led to significant economic challenges; principal among them, low industrial output, poverty, inequality, and unemployment.

The good news, however, is that there is a change of flow taking place in Africa with regards to how power is managed. A new crop of leaders has begun to rise to the centre who appreciate the need to move beyond the old ways. They are learning to accept the limitations they possess, which constitute the strength possessed by others who may not be within their immediate circles. We are seeing governance systems across Africa transforming as capable and deserving youth, women, the disabled, and previously excluded experts are now coming to the table and playing a role in shaping a better Africa. This kind of thinking is not new, it is tried, tested and proven.

When Moses led the children of God across the Red Sea from slavery to freedom, he assumed absolute power. He was doing everything, to the extent that he almost forgot his wife and two sons. He forgot about his legacy and the future of Israel as a nation. Thank God for a wise father-in-law, Jethro, who decided to share the wisdom that had long been adopted by African governments of the day and had proven effective. He advised Moses to share power and responsibility with other competent and capable individuals who would share his vision for a better future.

How the Flow is Shifting

Moses had been too busy and focused on the task at hand and had no time to think about another method of administering differently. It started slowly and easy, but as time went on it became too cumbersome; unfortunately for Moses, he could not see that he was failing to run his government effectively. Jethro brought the new FLOW in power. He confronted him with a truth: this thing you are doing is not right; look among your people, you have capable leaders right here. Give them assignments to assist you so that both you and the people will be happy.

We are living in a similar epoch on the continent. Our leaders are starting to appreciate that the competence and expertise we need is abundantly available amongst our people. Emerging leaders are beginning to realise that the old ways are not taking us where we are going, so there is a positive change of leadership. As this flow continues democratically, we are about to experience cleaner, smarter, and more effective leadership systems emerging from this great continent. Our leaders are becoming more consultative in their approach and as a result the quality of ideas that are driving our progress are improving successively. This has been made possible because all the years of suffering and deprivation led our people to their knees in prayer. With such investments in prayer, God has responded with solid leaders that are emerging on various levels. These are not just village and tribal leaders, but world-class leaders who will transform the world by transforming Africa.

Emerge Now
"But if thou altogether holdeth thy peace at this time, then shall there enlargement and deliverance arise to the Jews from another place, but thou and thy father's house shall be destroyed, and who knoweth whether thou art come, to the kingdom for such a time as this"

Esther 4:14

Now is the time to come out of hiding, face the risks associated and play your role. No one is going to do what you were born to do. This is not the time for assumptions, and fear but a time to step up and step into the leadership void. To change the flow, we need exceptional leadership on levels, from personal, family, tribal, community, civic, organisational, institutional, industrial, national and continental level. Every one of us was born with a specific assignment from God; by finding out what it is and delivering what you were born for, you are taking your God-ordained place of leadership in the world. The leaders we need are those who dare to lead from where they are now. Do not wait to be a member of parliament before you start to lead. Lead from where you are. As a street cleaner, lead through excellence and work ethic, the streets that you clean must be the best in your city. If you polish shoes, you must be the best there is in the world. If you clean cars, do it in such a way that they will never find anybody who does it like you anywhere. There are enough resources on this continent to remove poverty completely. What we need to achieve is a transformed leadership paradigm.

When we have successfully shifted the flow of ideas, wealth, and power Africa will begin to shine like a city built on a hill. What is exciting is that young Africans are beginning to see the big picture, and we need to drive this momentum and shift these three fundamental flows in our favour.

PART II

MINDSHIFT

CHAPTER FIVE

A NEW PARADIGM

—⌁—

"The present convergence of crises – in money, energy, education, health, water, soil, climate, politics, the environment, and more – is a birth crisis, expelling us from the old world into a new"
Charles Eisenstein

I am a lover of nature, rivers to be precise. Their currency, force, and velocity intrigue me. I often wonder what the actual volumes of megalitres flowing past a place at any given moment are. It is beyond my finite mind to fathom and calculate now, but for the experts, I know it is a piece of cake. I think of the Nile River, Africa's longest channel and wonder how much water flows and courses through it without cessation. The Congo River, the Zambezi River and the River Niger also come to mind. One cannot help but be enamoured by the torrential flow of these channels as they thunder like a mighty rushing wind throughout the continent. It seems crazy to even imagine that there was a day in time when these rivers did not exist. To think that many centuries back, none of these rivers even existed, until God spoke a word and the tide turned. Suddenly, trickles emerged and slowly they penetrated through the cracks and they began to build momentum until an entire river was born. A river that would stretch and connect multiple locations and bless many villages with life-giving substance. Sprawling communities that would build around its pathway as the river created opportunities for livelihoods to be improved. Technological advancements that were realised in the form of hydroelectric power stations and the tourist attractions that were born in the majestic and picturesque views the landscape presented to the appreciating eye because of the flow. Imagine how one word spoken by God brought forth this wondrous flow that would unlock so much blessing to those inhabitants who occupy the lands around the flow.

As I mentioned earlier, Africa is blessed to be the fountain where the rivers that nourish the global economy emanate. Meaning a lot of what is currently keeping the world ticking is coming from our soil, soul, and sweat. The sad news is that the continent occupies the bottom of the pyramid when it comes to benefitting from its magnanimous flows. Just as the rivers connect sources to the mouths that need what the flow has to offer, Africa's strategic geographic position connects it to every other continent with ease, allowing her to bless the nations with her flows in a unique way that no other continent can boast to. When one looks at all the continents, we are at the centre of them all, and we are equally central in global economic flows. If our eyes could open to this reality, we will be able to maximise the flows of Africa in our favour.

Two Ways of Seeing the Future

Every one of us has a worldview. It is the paradigm or the lens through which we each see the world. This explains why different people see things differently. I think there are two ways of seeing the world. This illustration will explain what I mean. After one marathon race, the sponsors had brought in huge boxes containing hamburgers for the participants. After crossing the line, runners would join the queue to get to the point where they could choose the type of burgers they wanted. Two friends who were running together arrived and found the line was long; one friend was not willing to stand in the queue for so long, while the other friend was not willing to miss out on a free burger. The discussion between the two continued for a while until one of them decided to sit under the tree and the other went close to where the burger boxes were. *"Excuse me!"* he said while stretching his hand into the box and came out with a burger. It was not the chicken burger he wanted but a beef burger, and as he munched going towards the shade where his friend was resting, he mumbled the words, *"This was a good choice after all!"* He did not get the choice of burger he wanted, but he got the food he needed without standing in the queue. The lesson in this story is that one friend was so discouraged by the long line of runners who wanted food, but he was too tired to stand in the queue for food. The other friend wanted the food so much that he came up with a strategy to get his burger without standing in the queue for long. This is the kind of paradigm shift we need in Africa today. It is time we lay aside the excuses born out of our past experiences and the old narrative that told us we are incapable of turning the fortunes of our continent around and deal a decisive blow to the social and economic ills that have entangled us for very long. We must shift away from the old mindset that drives us to send our begging bowls all over the world in search of aid and adopt a new paradigm. We must take charge of our situation and devise practical and implementable strategies that can radically transform our future.

The Old vs The New

"And he spake also a parable unto them; No man putteth a piece of a new garment upon an old; if otherwise, then both the new maketh a rent, and the piece that was taken out of the new agreeth not with the old."

Luke 5:36

For very long Africa has been under the siege of multinationals that control the global markets of Africa's most precious resources. Our economies have been for very long forced to be price takers who have little say in the evolution of the global markets and industries we supply our resources to. Sadly, Africa continues

to supply these resources in their primary state without beneficiation, earning low prices, importing the refined products back as
high-value goods. The net effect of which favours the middlemen,
who are oftentimes of Western or Eastern domicile, and disadvantages the producer, who in this case is the African. Most times, we
must accept the short end of the stick because the barriers and the
obstacles facing us are prohibitive to our prosperity and growth.
We have horticultural giants domiciled in the Netherlands and
listed on various exchanges in the West, who produce flowers in
our nations and expropriate the profits they generate from our
continents, back to their homelands, investing very little into the
spring. These corporations leave us barren to contend with our
perennial challenges such as poverty, inequality, and youth unemployment. When our indigenous agricultural entrepreneurs at-
tempt to enter the same industry and markets, they are met with
insurmountable obstacles such as lack of capital, poor access to
markets, and ridiculous and frustrating red tape. They are eventually forced to fold as they fail to access prime markets because
they are just not welcome to the party. Many have been subject-
ed to mafia-type price wars that made their operations unviable.
It is an exclusive big boys club made up of beneficiaries of our
resources. Africans are only entertained at the dinner table if we
agree to sit as lapdogs who are content waiting for the crumbs
that fall from the big boy's table.

A New Way of Thinking

I am not highlighting this reality to create a pity party or a
protest that will yield no realisable fruit. I am mentioning this to
challenge the African, as the indigenous steward of God's fountain, to think out of the box, innovate, and see how we can leverage the fountain and the flow to bring prosperity to our own.
Africa needs a new paradigm. It is time we do away with old patterns of doing business. Traditional approaches which were a simple copy and paste from the East or West will not cut it anymore.
We need to be thinking about how we are going to build indus-

tries around our natural resources, human capital potential, and the linkages we share regionally, continentally, and globally. We need to see how we can create sustainable competitive advantage around our strengths and opportunities. How are we going to neutralise our weaknesses, overcome the threats and barriers that stand between what Africa has been blessed with, and the markets that need and value what we offer? Do we need to improve our investment climate so we can attract more capital with fewer strings attached? Should we invest in the exploration of new greenfield markets that are going to deal with our people on more favourable terms? Maybe we need to renegotiate trade agreements amongst ourselves and create our very own centralised regional and continental market hubs for goods that the rest of the world demands from Africa. Think about it, a gold exchange in Sandton, South Africa, or in Accra, Ghana, or a diamond exchange in Mutare, Zimbabwe or Kinshasa, DRC, where a huge percentage of our continental production will be bought, sorted, and sold after beneficiation and refining. Just as we do with tobacco and the sales of many exports.

Must-Have Skill

The Future of Jobs Report published by the World Economic Forum states identifies problem solving, critical thinking and creativity, as the top three must-have skills in the Fourth Industrial Revolution. Innovation is the result of exercising these skills and it is a critical competence and culture we must develop among our people. Our youthful and creative population is an asset we can leverage as the Fourth Industrial Revolution gains momentum. We need to arm and equip our people to turn away from whining and complaining. We need to empower them to be creative and innovative in solving the myriad challenges that stand between us and our *kairos* opportunity. Africa needs its exceptional minds; our Daniels, Josephs, and Davids, to rise and solve the complexities that are frustrating the ability of our people to harness the flows of wealth and power running through our continent from Cape to Cairo, and from our Atlantic shores to those of the Indian Ocean.

Africa's Superhighway
"Broadband is as important as building roads"
~Alain Nkontchou, Ecobank Chairman

One of the greatest infrastructural developments to hit Africa in the last decade or so is the laying of fibre optic technology across the entire continent. Many analysts and forecasters see this as the game-changer Africa needs to create more inclusive growth and hopefully, shared and common prosperity. In this digital age, the more countries, cities, institutions, villages, communities, households, and individuals we connect to the network, the more opportunities we are creating to onboard more and more people into the flow of the digital age. Our future is one where blockchain, the internet of things, artificial intelligence, machine learning, and drones are going to be centre stage, it is good that Africa is creating this super digital highway that will link every inch of the continent to the digital world. The innovations that this development will unlock are going to see us limit the amount of revenue we channel to other parts of the world in search of solutions. Instead, we will be better positioned to create exportable solutions that we see the tide of global flows turn in our favour, we just must be wise and shrewd about it.

It is Already Happening

A young man from Rwanda by the name Israel Pimbe exemplifies what I mean. Through his company Zipline International, Israel has developed a Fourth Industrial Revolution oriented business. Zipline runs the world's first autonomous drone delivery system that delivers medical supplies to health care facilities in the remote areas of Rwanda and Ghana at a national scale. Through this innovation, Zipline has been able to solve the health care challenges that we had normalised on the continent. Zipline also operates an artificial intelligence innovation which allows patients living in remote areas to access specialist treatment at their primary health care facility. This removes the need to transport patients to referral hospitals for consultations. African innovation is collapsing barriers to the flow of not only wealth, ideas, and power, even the barriers to access to quality health care treatment by more and more people. Indeed, the tide is turning.

Africa's New Cape to Cairo

We need to innovatively confront and collapse the barriers to intra-Africa and global trade and ensure that the solutions created will have a downstream effect and impact on our communities. We need to pull down the barriers that slow down our progress and delay our imminent destiny. Africa needs to allow the Joshuas and Calebs among us to lead us victoriously against the giants occupying our land of promise, which is flowing with milk and honey. We need leaders who will confront the elephant in the room and renegotiate treaties, charters, and trade agreements to remove the bottlenecks and break the heavy yokes that have been choking us for so long, so we can finally breathe.

Our ability to harness the flow depends greatly on us identifying the threats to our prosperity as a continent and addressing them innovatively. We need to deal with porous borders and tighten the security of our financial gateways so we can minimise the leakages that have been bleeding our economies dry for centuries. We need to deal decisively with pirates who threaten the security of cargo in transit and be equally decisive in dealing with the poverty and greed that fuels these activities. Africa needs to take advantage of technology and improve national, regional, and continental infrastructure so the cost of doing business with us comes down. This will activate local investment and attract foreign direct investment, stimulate our local economies, lower unemployment, and drive competitive value-added exports. Our continent needs us to improve financial market depth by integrating of our continental capital markets and accelerating the establishment of regional and continental bourses. This will create opportunities for homegrown solutions to be incubated on African soil without the burden of having to pay the bulk of our dividends and interest beyond our shores.

A Case for Agility and Adaptation

I am yet to see a river that flows in a straight line. Regardless of its magnanimity, every river must adapt to its terrain. The river's commitment is to continually flow into a stream larger than itself and make its contribution to the greater good. A river will not be stopped in its mission and commitment by anything not even trees, rocks, valleys, mountain ranges, and gorges. Rivers can navigate the landscape with agility and finesse because their role is to avail themselves in the service of mankind at a household, community, city, provincial, national, and regional levels depending on the size of the river. The presence of this flow does not guarantee automatic benefit to regions that it flows through. Those territories and people who are privileged to enjoy the flow must learn how to harness the flow by being innovative around it. It is this thinking that brought about hydroelectric power. The understanding that every flow can be channelled to create multi-level benefits to the societies along its path is needed if we are to accelerate our growth and development. The same river that is providing power for industrialisation is also providing fishing opportunities, irrigation potential, transportation of goods and people, tourist experiences, and whatever else we can innovate out of the flow.

In the same way, imagine if we began to innovate more around the flows of gas, oil, gold, diamonds, agricultural fertility, a youthful skilled and educated population, and the gross domestic product under our feet. We would turn the tide of the flow in our favour in no time and become the African paradise we are destined to be.

Africa has all it needs to industrialise and evolve into a mega economy. The tide has already begun to rise in our favour and our *kairos* moment is upon us. What we need is to stretch our minds and think of how we can unlock value through innovation. We need to adopt a new paradigm of thought, a perspective that sees opportunities and not just obstacles, possibilities and not just problems.

From Peaks to Plains: A New Mindset Going Forward

When we look at migration patterns globally and even within our nations and continent, we will observe the general direction is from low places to the peaks of civilisations - rural to urban, underdeveloped to developed, and from places of less opportunity to those were opportunities are seen to be low hanging and more abundant. This pattern of migration is unhealthy and chokes the spread of development. It limits and stifles innovation. When people live concentrated in these peaks, they become a greater burden on the economy and its infrastructure as resources and opportunities become concentrated in these centres of advancement. This chokes the flow and makes it difficult to spread wealth and access to opportunity. This explains the brain drain that continues to cripple Africa's prospects for a resurgence. We have entrenched a mindset that runs away from problems and challenges and seeks to find comfort in more developed cities and nations. This culture has killed our ability to face our challenges head-on and innovate to solve them.

Africa needs to dump the narrative that says wealth is found in the West or the city. Real wealth is found anywhere you find yourself on the African continent. While you might not have adequate and world-class infrastructure, but under your feet is the flow of wealth that nations and transnational corporations fight to control. But here we are creating a vacuum of talent by sending all our sharpest thinkers to go and build other nations and economies, while those same nations come and occupy the springs of our wealth, from our mines, oil and gas deposits, our arable land and more.

A Vision for Shared Prosperity

To capture the tide and change the direction and results of the flow African governments now need to develop a new paradigm for inclusive development and wealth creation that will change the direction of human capital movement from one that under-develops our continent, regions, nations, and communities, to one that stimulates more continental, regional, national, and local economic development initiatives around our natural resources at a grassroots level. We need to cast a vision to build more special economic hubs and zones, towns, and cities around the industries that we can build around our resources. This will allow us to spread the wealth to the lowest levels in a more empowering and sustainable way and improve access to better services for our people everywhere. Let us endeavour to make the continent flatter, so that the cake can be enjoyed by more and more of our people by industrialising and making the development of paramount importance. This will enhance our ability to connect and collaborate across political, tribal, national, and racial divides. A good example is using agriculture to industrialise our village economies by adding markets, agro-based manufacturing, logistics support, mobile technology services, relevant financial services, and improved social services facilities. We can easily leverage investment into these local economies as we form them into special economic zones that offer tax incentives and a more favourable investment climate. This will raise the productive capacity of local economies to harness the flows that are already taking place there. It will also attract more skills, development, investment, and economic activity into the area making them more competitive and attractive as destinations for capital. This will improve the competitiveness of the local agricultural industry and may even see an increase in the volumes produced over time and can even become an export centre in a few years. This will reduce the potential for brain drain and allow the benefits of the flows to be distributed in a more broad-based manner. More jobs and opportunities can be created, and the communities become more self-sustaining and organised. Our people's skills and expertise are also enhanced by such a change in flow.

Innovative Entrepreneurship

In a world, as interconnected as ours, we should be finding creative and innovative ways to connect the talents and abilities of our people to markets that will pay a decent premium on their work. A simple example can be the arts and crafts sector. We have so many talented young men and women in so many of our rural areas who can handcraft enviable accessories and sculpture that can be sold globally via the internet. These products are made using locally acquired stones, but the beauty and majesty are from the hands that make them, and they are a wonder to behold. We need to invest in developing the entrepreneurial capabilities of such young people by affording them the training, opportunities, and platforms they need to gain access to prime markets for their prime work. We must empower the arts industry to think entrepreneurially, strategically, and globally. It would lovely to see accessories handcrafted by our youth in a village deep in Central or West Africa being sold for hundreds and thousands of euros in Frankfurt, Germany, with the producer making the most in the whole transaction.

The Untelevised Revolution

Africa has been experiencing booms that we never hear about in the global media space. You hardly ever hear of the many young African entrepreneurs who have successfully built businesses that have whet the appetites of the highly discerning Silicon Valley based venture capitalists and fund managers. Entities like Paystack, which provides online payment and transfer solutions for Africa, have been able to raise capital from Visa International to the tune of $8 million. Paystack runs an integrated API (Application Programming Interface) which connects hundreds of thousands of businesses within Nigeria and is already responsible for 15% of all online payments within the nation and is looking to expand its footprint continentally and has its sights on competing for a greater share of the global market.

I believe we can create such possibilities by learning to think outside the box more. By choosing to rewrite our own story and becoming masters of our destiny, we can surely create new possibilities for Africa by creating a culture of innovation.

Growing to Our Next Level

It is very comfortable to go with the flow; there are fewer conflicts and fewer obstacles. The only challenge is that there will never be growth and transformation. The fear of changing that flow is real and it cannot happen until and unless we are willing to take a risk; transformation comes only through risk-taking. We can only grow when we choose to swim upstream against the grain of the current flow. All the innovations we see and enjoy today are a result of individuals who grew tired of the status quo and took the risk to do the unusual and the not-so-obvious.

To access to the next level of life, we must keep moving, even against the flow of adversity. When I was a child learning to count numbers, it was very scary to read beyond five, yet it was exciting to read up to ten. I celebrated so much to count to ten because I overcame the adversity and challenges associated with transcending the number five. What I did not know was that there were other numbers to count beyond ten, and that was the scariest obstacle in my life at that level. How could someone leave the ten that you have struggled for so long to master, and risk starting again? That did not make sense to me, so it was a huge struggle. Most people get stuck here and they die here. If we are not willing to give up the ten, we can never go to eleven; at the next level, there is an increase with one and soon, the experience of the previous level accelerates our growth to more and bigger things in life. We cannot love ten to the degree that we give up going to eleven. If we stop going, we will stop growing.

Growing Pains

All growth is painful. It requires that we dissociate from the old and familiar and embrace the new and foreign. In the book of Exodus 14: 4–9, it is written that the children of Israel left Egypt to go to the Promised Land flowing with milk and honey, but it was not a walk in the park. The same God who said to Pharaoh, *"Let my people go!"* also hardened their hearts to follow them. Our old ways, mindsets, habits, and values will always seek to keep us chained to them, thereby inhibiting and limiting our ability to adopt a new paradigm. This makes growth and evolution painful. Hence, God allows some things to keep chasing us to keep us fresh, relevant, and motivated to grow.

The next level is only realised when we leave the present and move on to the unfamiliar. Of course, we must navigate through some turbulent transitions, which will involve seasons of uncertainty, but when we do get to the other side, we would have evolved in our thinking and worldview. We will never know who we are until we have liberated ourselves from the current paradigms we hold. The old and archaic keep us chained to the inhibiting and restricting narratives of yesterday. We need to embrace a new paradigm that is influenced by a biblical and prophetic understanding of Africa and her destiny.

As we journey towards our next, we must keep moving and resist the temptation of stagnation. We must brace ourselves to overcome the frustrations that come with change and adopt a new paradigm. We will grasp some things faster than others. New forms thinking and behaving will demand more from us than we are comfortable with, but that must not stop us. We must fight the pressure of going back to the old paradigms. We must overcome our fear of an unknown future and embrace the unfamiliar, for therein lies our destiny and promise.

Forward Ever, Backwards Never

To the discerning and spiritual the ways of God are always simple and within our reach. The breakthrough of the nation of Israel was in the hands of Moses, yet he did not realise it at the time. When they arrived at the Red Sea, reality was staring them in the face; it was impossible to cross and it was also real that the strong chariots and horsemen of Pharaoh were approaching fast. Now, they heard God say, *"these Egyptians that you see now you will see them no more"*. That must have been very difficult to process. God instructed Moses to stretch forth his rod over the sea; a strong east wind came to divide the water and caused the sea-bed to dry up, and they walked on dry ground. The strong east wind caused the flow of the sea to change as the victorious children of Israel walked to other side. This did not deter the enemy because God had hardened their hearts so that they should pursue the children of Israel no matter what. God had another agenda for both the Egyptians and the children of Israel. When Moses and the entire nation had crossed the sea, they began to praise God. They had left the familiar and the old and had entered the new. It was then that Moses was instructed to point the rod over the sea and the waters started closing, washing away the Egyptians and their chariots, confirming to the Israelites that what God had promised had come to pass and they cannot go back there again. They went in as slaves and came out as sons. By transitioning through the Red Sea, Israel was detaching from an old way of life and adopting a new and unfamiliar paradigm altogether.

Leading Africa Deeper into the Unknown

Leading in these times excites me. We are venturing into the deep unknown. We are moving towards what we have never known or experienced. Whenever men embark on such escapades, there is no map or reference point to follow, the voice within becomes the only compass that is needed to reach our destination. These are the leaders we need in such an epoch as the one we are in. Yes, we learn from history and other civilisations but more importantly, we must follow the leading of the Spirit of God into our future. We need leaders who will operate in sync with the seasons of the Lord, who are committed to ensuring Africa is syncopated with the calendar of heaven. Just as Moses led the nation of Israel out of Egypt into the wilderness before handing over to Joshua, who led them into the land of promise, we need such women and men to emerge on the continent. Leaders who will not rest until they have fulfilled the assignment upon their lives.

One of my heroes in the Bible is the man called Abraham. In Genesis chapter 12, it is recorded that he was told by God to leave his country and his people and go to a country that he did not know. Clearly, this shows that the purposes of God in Abraham's life were not going to materialise if he remained in his comfort zone - the place of his birth and among his relatives. To preserve future generations and the clear plans of God that were invested in Abraham, God had to take him away to an unfamiliar place. Leaving the familiar is never easy, but it is never to destroy us. It will always bring the best out of us. Detaching from the old is painful but gainful. What is even scarier is when we must operate in the limbo of not being who and where we used to be, and not yet fully transitioned into who and where we are called to be. This becomes the leadership challenge of navigating from the old towards the new. We are confronted by a lot of volatility, uncertainty, complexity, and ambiguity (VUCA), but when we hold on to the promise of God and we lead with courage as we follow the inner compass of the Holy Spirit we will make it to the other side.

Fine Tuning

Leading in VUCA times is very challenging, hence many sabotage their assignment by settling for mediocrity, which is far below God's intent and purpose. To lead effectively in such times, the leader must take time to search out and know what God would have them do. Gaining clarity is no walk in the park. There are too many voices and narratives competing with the voice of God, making it very difficult to hear clearly and lead with certainty in uncertainty. Every now and again as a leader you need to separate yourself from the noise of everyday life, the media, think tanks, research reports, projections, and forecasts and tune in to the frequency of the Spirit. Take a holiday and allow yourself an opportunity to refocus, recreate, and receive new energy for the next level.

Familiarity can wear you out and slow you down. It can cause interference to your ability to receive the purposes of God for your life, family, organisation, industry, nation, and/or continent, depending on your level of leadership and assignment. So, to explore your destiny and purpose, you need to leave the familiar and experience the unfamiliar. God was able to take Abraham into the blessing and make him the custodian of the blessings of the future generations, which would not have happened had he remained in the old familiar place where he had resorted to worshipping idols like the rest of his people were doing.

A giant and courageous step into unfamiliar territory is needed to lay hold of our blessing and the legacy of the next generation. The next giant step could be taking a new course, degree, and qualification, finding a coach or mentor, reading a new book, visiting and talking to a different people group, or creating or inventing a new product; or a new industry, a new development agenda for Africa, there is no limit to what can be done, especially considering the needs out there. Anything that will bring success in life will meet the need of people.

Leading into the unknown will also challenge you to embrace deeper levels of diversity. So, go ahead and enjoy human diversity; learn about the many cultures, races, languages, and values of the many different ethnicities on the continent and celebrate the variety of the magnificent continent. The highest form of ignorance is displayed in all forms of discrimination, be it racial, gender, generational, tribal, national, or ethnic. It is time African people embrace and celebrate their diversity. Strangely, children up to primary school levels do not see colour. But what happens as they grow up? The familiar creeps in and suddenly, discrimination surfaces.

Constant and Continuous Improvement

Japan was a poverty-stricken country with little hope for recovery from the destruction of the Second World War. The nation went on to make certain critical changes in how they operated. They chose to demilitarise and industrialise. In this process, they developed an interesting concept, which has become a global phenomenon called *"kaizen"*. *Kaizen* is a Japanese philosophy that is built around constant and never-ending improvement. It is founded upon the idea that improvement must be continuous and that nothing is ever at its peak and as such must be improved upon regularly. Everything that is, can be refined and improved upon if we are willing to push the boundaries and think beyond our pre-set parameters. This philosophy is the secret behind their ability to overtake the United States as the leader in the global automotive industry and many other industrial sectors.

Improvement of anything in life comes from constant and continuous movement: in practising for a game, in our walk with God, and in our relationships. It is critical to know that we are always more than we think. The best of you is ahead of you! I love it when the Bible confirms this truth in Jeremiah 29:11, *"I know the thoughts that I have for you, thoughts for the good and not for the bad, to give you hope and an expected future."* It is clear God is not talking about them in the present, but He is talking about them in the future. Our tomorrow is much better than our today; there is more to come that is more exciting and bigger than whatever may seem big and exciting now.

We must develop the consistency that unlocks the peak of our fruitfulness. Consistency is the evidence of maturity and the pathway to mastery. The difference between an amateur and a professional is consistency. The professional level is the evidence that practice sessions were taken diligently, consistently, and continually.

Consistent practice develops a rhythm. Life is about rhythm.

That is why we have seasons, months, weeks and days. We have marriages, pregnancies, school, work and home. The Bible talks about seasons: a time to embrace and time to refrain from embracing, a time to sow and a time to reap, a time to laugh and a time to cry, there is a time to be born and there is a time to die (Eccl. 3: 1–8). These cycles evidence the rhythm of life that we need to appreciate, embrace, and master. So, the correct rhythms of life must be followed to reap the best from life; otherwise, the opposite will prevail.

The best way of describing the correct and the wrong rhythms of life are divinely put together in the book of Psalms, chapter 1: 1–3:

"Blessed is the man that walketh not in the counsel of the ungodly, nor standeth   in the way of the sinners, nor sitteth in the seat of the scornful. 2 But his delight is in the of the LORD, and in his law doth he meditates day and night. 3 And he shall be like a tree planted by the rivers of water, that bringeth forth his fruit in his season, his leaf also shall not wither, and whatsoever he doeth shall prosper."

This is the pattern for living a successful life that God has given us; therefore, it is important to come out of self-imposing and destructive rhythms as a continent. Consistency must be practised habitually until we break the destructive cycles and rhythms and establish the correct ones. Once we achieve that, we must keep the momentum going as we build velocity. The velocity of consistency brings prosperity and continuous birthing of creative ideas that will bring more prosperity and ultimately leaves us in a continuous cycle of blessings. It is easy to see pitfalls when our rhythm is going because if we fall but cannot stay down. We will stumble but we will get up and keep walking. The difference between a dream and reality is consistency and commitment to continuous and never-ending improvement, *kaizen*.

CHAPTER SIX

GENERATION NEXT:
RAISING THE LEADERS OF TOMORROW

—⌘—

*"The significant problems we face can never be solved by the same
level of thought that created them"*
Albert Einstein

Emerging on the continent and set to coincide with Africa's rising
tide are two generations, the first being the millennials or Generation Y, (born between 1982 and 1994), and the other being the
post-millennial generation or Generation Z, (born between 1995
and 2010). These two generations were mostly born and raised in
Africa's post-independent era. Most have never experienced the
brutality of colonialism and are coming into their own at a time
when the continent is ripening. They have however been subject-
ed to the frustration of growing up in an Africa led by our liberators who lacked the skill sets and mindsets for good governance
and building states that are strong and resilient to the many economic and social shocks that confront us in our times. They are
a generation that is generally dissatisfied and restless. They are
desperately agitating for change and a transformation of the status quo. Exasperated by being talented and yet excluded from
platforms that allow them to express their potential they are demanding a landscape that allows them to pursue their dreams,

purposes, and passions, and be globally competitive. These two generations do not look at the challenges that face our continent as insurmountable. Instead, they see the complexities of Africa as opportunities for inventiveness and solution creation. They do not think like their predecessors do. They possess a vision for Africa to be the central global player that she has potential of becoming. They have been asking some very difficult and uncomfortable questions about our present status in the global scheme of things. Examples of the crucial and yet uncomfortable questions I have been humbled to be asked include, why is Africa in possession of real wealth and yet we are called poor? How do we turn the tide so that Africa's wealth is held by Africans and benefit Africans in a more evident way? Why do we look East and West and never look inward for homegrown solutions?

To quote the co-founder of Paystack the Nigerian based online payment solutions company, Shola Akinlade, *"It takes a lot of nuances to build for African businesses."* He represents the thinking that is dominant amongst the two emerging generations. They are not steeped in the victim narrative that typified us for generations. Blaming colonialism, civil wars, tribalism, corruption, and the many issues we have often blamed for our challenges. They see their African roots, experience, and presence as a source of competitive advantage, which puts them ahead of any competitor for the African market. They have chosen a new lens to look at our continent through. Like David, when he heard of Goliath threats, they have chosen to respond differently from the old generation. They have chosen to take up the challenge and deal decisively with the giants that have been restricting the flow that should be blessing them as a people. These generations represent the new wineskins that will be able to contain the new flow of wine that God is releasing upon Africa.

Defining Africa's Future Leadership

When we analyse the generations that are set to benefit greatly from Africa's boom and emergence, we will notice that they possess traits that I find exciting and promising. One cannot help but light up with hope. Our Generations Y and Z show promise that we must harness and channel to the favour of our continent, lest we lose them to more advanced economies as has been the historical backdrop. The following is not an exhaustive list but one that highlights the most evident and promising traits that we cannot help but be attentive to if we are to effectively set Africa up for her *kairos*.

1. Digital Natives who Possess Technological Mastery

Africa's Generation Y and Z have grown up in an era when mobile phones and technology are both ubiquitous and universal. With that came exposure and mastery of mobile technology, the internet, and all that can be derived from it. From sparking hashtag movements that have seen despotic and oppressive regimes fall, to creating businesses that have a reach that transcends their locales, the youth of Africa have redefined the playing field in all areas through digital mastery.

Digital innovation is creating unprecedented opportunities for Africa to grow its economy, create jobs, transform people's lives, open new and endless possibilities, and leapfrog us going forward into a brighter future for our continent and youth. Intending to digitally connect every individual, business, and government in Africa by 2030, the African Union, with the support of the World Bank Group, has embarked on an ambitious journey—a *"moon-shot"* - that will help African countries accelerate progress in bringing high-speed connectivity to all, and laying the foundations for a vibrant digital economy. This is an imperative effort which we cannot afford to miss out on because the African millennial is a digital native who requires this infrastructure to be in place, so they can be set to bring transformation to the continent and the world. While this is a welcome development, the youth of Africa feel that 2030 is too far and I agree. They need universal and affordable connectivity now, and we must crack our heads and develop the correct mix of private and public partnership that will deliver this number one human right of the 21st century to every household in the shortest possible time.

2. Freethinking Creatives who Have No Qualms about Pushing Boundaries

The youth of Africa seem to have no sacred cows or a sense of loyalty to traditions and systems, particularly the ones that are responsible for stagnating the growth of our continent. They are open-minded and are looking outside their mental and conceptual borders to push their agenda forward. I was inspired by African start-ups coming out of Rwanda, South Africa, Ghana, Nigeria, Ethiopia, Tanzania, Kenya, and many more of our nations. These innovations are challenging the boundaries, knocking down barriers, disrupting the unmitigated outflow of money from our shores, and positioning Africa to tap into the global economy as an equal partner. This is being achieved across a broad plethora of industries ranging from education, healthcare, technology, finance, and agriculture.

The youth will no longer accept the cheap political rhetoric of yesteryear. They have little respect for the giants that have sought to keep us from taking possession of the land that is flowing with milk and honey. Instead, they are innovating radically to solve the challenges that face us. Examples include entities like Hello Tractor, which partnered with John Deere, a US based tractor maker, to provide an "über-type" service to over 250,000 farmers in Nigeria. In so doing, Hello Tractor has alleviated the pressure upon budding and emerging farmers to own their tractor. This innovation has collapsed a barrier that has kept so many from pursuing farming because of a lack of adequate capital. It is true that this generation truly thinks where there is no box at all.

3. Passion for Learning

Our world is a fast-changing and ever-evolving one, and the

last decade has proven to be one where change has been happening at an accelerated pace. Some would suggest that it is happening at the speed of thought. Unlike the boomers, who prefer the world to remain static for them to maintain a sense of relevance, the youth of Africa have no deceptions relating to the world they live in. They appreciate that to attain and maintain relevance in this age of continual disruption, there is a need for constant and never-ending learning and development. Now, this does not mean they are always in universities and institutions of higher learning, but they are constantly engaged in various forms of personal growth and development initiatives. They are always adding new skills to their lives. The term *"side hustle"* has become so popular among them, it is now mainstream. Many of our young people are adding new skills to their portfolio and using them to make money on the side, sometimes even going as far as making their side hustle their major stream of income.

They just refuse to stop learning because they love and appreciate the value of improvement in this information age. They appreciate that learning is the gateway to opportunity, and it improves one's competitiveness in a world or market that may not be willing to make room for them. It is not uncommon to hear of them taking online courses at Harvard, Coursera, Udemy, Yale, Cambridge, University of Cape Town, and the many elite institutions of learning.

4. Entrepreneurial

A 2015 study carried out by the Global Entrepreneurship Monitor (GEM) and Youth Business International (YBI) showed that 60% of the Africans polled were optimistic about the availability of good business opportunities, and believed they had the skills and knowledge to start and run a business. This compares to just over 17% of young people in the European Union, almost 17% in the Asia Pacific and South Asia regions, and around 30% in North America. The only other region that came close to

Sub-Saharan Africa's optimism was Latin America and the Caribbean, where 40% of the youth believed they had the opportunities, skills, and knowledge to start and run a small business. This is according to the January 2015 report titled, *"Understanding the entrepreneurial attitudes, aspirations and activities of young people"*.

The report detailed the attitudes, aspirations, and activities of the youth, and we can all see that the emerging generation looks at life and business differently from their predecessors. With Africa's youth unemployment standing at an unacceptable high of 40%, they appreciate that their future and destiny is in their hands, and they are determined to do something about it. Instead of looking at our statistics as reasons to be despondent they see them as growth and learning opportunities, which they are ready to leverage and milk for their entrepreneurial value.

Generations Y and Z's on the continent have a strong inclination towards risk. They have been very bold and explicit in voicing their frustrations over the pressure their predecessors place upon them to go for more secure and traditional careers, choosing instead to make a profit and changing the world while they are at it.

According to the African Tech Start-ups Funding Report 2019, there was a 47% increase in funding towards African start-ups and it is projected that very soon we could see over a US$1 billion invested annually in new tech ventures on the continent. Even though most of this money is concentrated around the major established tech-hubs of Africa - Nigeria, Kenya, South Africa, and Egypt, many other nations are starting to attract investment from all over the world. Truly the African youth is living in an era of great opportunity and they have the entrepreneurial wit to match.

Investing in Africa's Leaders of the Future
To successfully catch and ride this tidal wave that is rising on the continent, we need to be intentional about investing in the

potential and promise of our youth. Our youth possess the traits, agility, and vibrancy that is needed to maximise the tide. They have proven that they are as competitive as any other youth demographic in the world. This is further accentuated by the fact that they have less to work with compared to their Western and Eastern counterparts, and yet they show up and show themselves competent and capable at a global scale. It is high time policymakers, business, financial institutions, and various multilateral institutions, come together and support the development and empowerment of the next generation of Africa leaders.

Our youth are not seeking handouts from anyone. They are looking for leverage so they can reach for the stars that they have potential to hit.

Digitising the Continent as a Matter of Urgency

One of the best ways to ensure that Africa's youth is positioned for the rising tide is digitising the African continent as matter of urgency. The youth are ready to maximise the opportunities that digital presents to them, but the infrastructure and the policy dynamic is letting them down. We can never fully harness the potential of our youth and the promise of Africa until we open the floodgates of connectivity. As mentioned earlier, we need to brainstorm and come up with the fastest, most affordable, and most viable way to ensure that we deliver this vital service to all parts of Africa as matter of urgency. Rural and urban alike, we need to ensure that we flatten the continent as far as internet connectivity is concerned. This will open the floodgates that will allow our youth to be absorbed into the mainstream economy, which has become a digital one.

Restructuring Economies

Our current economic structures are primarily designed to cater for and secure the investments of the huge multinational companies. As we have highlighted in previous chapters, this is not working for us. We have seen our economies grow at some of the fastest rates globally and consistently so, but we have not been able to dent poverty and inequality in the process. This shows that even though we are doing certain things right, we need to re-think some structural issues. Africa needs to make some significant and wholesale changes so our youth can have greater participation in the economy. We need to redesign our investment policy framework to ensure that those who invest in Africa come in as partners and not just extractors and exploiters of resources. We need them to invest in the real empowerment of our communities and people with a focus on raising the generation to empowered to excel and achieve exploits economically.

I remember reading about how diamonds that are mined in Africa are cut and polished in Indian villages before being exported from India to Antwerp. This must be nipped as a matter of urgency. Diamond mining houses that wish to invest here, must invest in the training and skills development of our local youth and set up beneficiation centres locally, that are owned and operated in partnership with locals. This will allow us to add value to our exports, and in the same vein empower our communities to industrialise and create local economic booms that can lead to diversified economies at a localised level.

New Educational Systems

When we encountered the current covid-19 pandemic, analysts say the world was forced to leap at least five years into the future as far as digital is concerned. Many were forced to work and learn remotely, and with that more opportunities for Africa emerged. This shift is one the world is not going back on, the new normal and most of its elements are here to stay. Africa can no longer continue to allow our education systems to lag. We must reform them across the board to ensure relevance and advantage for our youth. With a great percentage of the world's population coming from Africa over the next few decades, average incomes in Africa increasing, and with the greater percentage of the world's youth coming from Africa, we are a key market for the world's goods and services but more importantly, we can be a key producer of global innovation, goods, and services for export to the nations. As a result, we must reform our educational sector to raise leaders for tomorrow's world. Our educational sector should be focused on raising thinkers who think critically, strategically, innovatively, globally, generationally, digitally, and beyond.

Our curricula need realignment to the new reality that is unfolding before us. The slave mentalities of educating our youth to look for jobs must be done away with and replaced with a mindset of problem-solving, critical thinking, and entrepreneurship.

Making Africa SMME friendly

Research has proven that one of the best ways to accelerate and stimulate economic growth and improve income equality is to create environments that inspire the establishment and the growth of small micro and medium enterprise development. It has worked in the USA, China, Singapore, South Korea, UK, India, Rwanda, Nigeria, Kenya and so many countries. It will work in anywhere in Africa where an enabling environment is developed. We need policy and institutional frameworks that encourage the SMME sector of our continent to thrive. The ease of doing business must improve as a matter of urgency. Young people should not struggle to register and operate a business. The cost must come down and the red tape must be reduced to a bare minimum. Capital for start-ups should be widely accessible for viable ideas. Our financial services sector needs to be reformed so they not only serve existing businesses but the emerging entrepreneurs in both urban and rural areas.

Africa needs to develop more incubations hubs and accelerator programs for new businesses especially those founded and operated by women and youth. A continental youth-focused stock market is needed, and more venture capital funds and angel investor platforms that have greater risk orientation are a necessity.

Allowing the Entrepreneurial to Lead and Government to Follow

Among the greatest frustrations and obstacles to our emergence as a continent, is a sluggish and slow government. It is as though our governments are in a maintenance mode when we need them to lead from the front. Our entrepreneurs are opportunity minded. They see where the world is going, and they have the solutions and mechanisms to get us there. However, our governments are more focused on implementing fossilised and antiquated ideas that have lost relevance due to fast-paced change. A simple example is how mobile telephony and clean energy have revolutionised the telecoms and power sector, respectively. In the nineties, governments owned and controlled these two sectors and were failing to roll out access to these vital communication and power needs of our people. When the mobile telephony revolution came to Africa, it grew faster on the continent than it did in many developed countries because innovators and entrepreneurs came up with lower-cost solutions to the challenges and assumed leadership in solving the problems. The same applies with energy, when the solar energy revolution came to our shores, we saw more communities electrified at a lower cost because the government allowed the entrepreneurs to take lead in areas where the government should not have been leading in the first place.

Imagine with me if the government was to allow entrepreneurs to lead in education, healthcare, waste management, and other key social services as they did with the two technologies I mentioned above, we would see a major leap in the improvements of the quality of life enjoyed by our people even in the most remote locations.

Raising Critical Thinkers

We must be deliberate about raising critical thinkers in the next generation. Part of the dilemma we face today is founded upon our inability to do so. Our leaders have oftentimes agreed to deals and trade agreements that were signed without much critical thought invested therein, owing to desperation and the pressure to deliver results to our restless populations. Being a critical thinker involves taking a closer look at the environment we are in, identifying the problems around us, and coming up with lasting solutions to help people progress to the next level of their lives. Critical thinking is about solving problems and inducing excitement in the people that we lead at family, society, and country levels. Our emerging young leaders must be trained to understand and decipher where we are now, what we want to be when we want to be that, how we are going to evolve into that, and the kinds of partnerships we need to get there.

A Rabbit Trail

One of the biggest challenges with our generation Y and Z today are the addictions of all sorts; the most impactful of these being social media. This has exposed them to narratives that they have adopted as truth without critically analysing them. This has brought a huge communication breakdown in our society that requires us to take drastic and urgent measures to help the next generation because the current generation is suffering from the effect of this problem already. Although the use of cell phones has made communication extremely effective, it has broken down person to person interaction, and with that our sense of humanity or what we on the continent called *ubuntu*. Nothing beats direct communication or eyeball- to-eye-ball conversation to bring huge unmatched excitement and bonding that brings families, communities, and people groups together and strengthens relations permanently.

Another challenge our society is going through now is that there is no empathy in the home environment, which has led to no sympathy at work, at school, on our roads, or in society at large. Parenting is being challenged like never before because there is no direct communication between father and mother or between father and child, and as a result, we have an insecure generation. Technology has changed people's perspectives; our children do not spend time with their parents because they are hooked up with people that are now influencing their thinking from diverse parts of the globe. They are glued to the small screen all day and have no need for parents except for clothes and food. This can negatively impact our ability to prepare the next generation adequately.

Everything we now need is instant, and there is no waiting period. Why cook if you can order? We used to wait for a taxicab to come, but now there is always an Uber two minutes away from us. These technological advancements have simplified life and have enhanced convenience, something we gladly embrace, but they have also entrenched an instant gratifying syndrome that has given birth to huge levels of impatience. While this represents a threat to our progress and development as people, it is an opportunity for a new generation of thinkers to rise and either revamp, customise, or create improved solutions that do not compromise our values as a people made in the image and likeness of God.

CHAPTER SEVEN

LIONESSES RISING

—∞—

*"their roaring shall be like a lioness, they shall roar like young
lions; yea, they shall roar, and lay hold of the prey, and carry it
away safe, and there shall be none to deliver.*
*And they shall roar against them in that day like the roaring of
the sea: and if one look unto the land, behold, darkness and dis-
tress; and the light is darkened in the clouds thereof."*
Isaiah 5:29

Alongside Africa's youth, our women represent the other untapped frontier of exponential growth. Statistic show that despite being the less supported gender in comparison to their male
counterparts, they are high potential demographic. With the economic landscape shifting every seven to ten years, women have
emerged not only as mainstream economic players but in many
cases as breadwinners and income anchors in households and nations. It would be folly for Africa to continue marginalising them
and their value. God created every human being in His image and
likeness. He created men and women as equals in potential, capacity, gifting and ability. Neither gender is superior, and none is
inferior to the other. Our roles may differ in the home as it pertains to husband and wife, but biblically that is as far as it goes.
Sadly, Africa has a history of neglecting this weapon of mass destruction to the many social and economic ills we face like pover-

ty, regression, and poor economic performance.

According to Ahunna Eziakonwa, Director of UNDP's Regional Bureau for Africa, it is estimated that since 2010 Africa has lost an estimated US$95 billion annually owing to gender disparity alone. Africa can never reach its peak if we do not unleash the gifts, talents, competences, resolve, leadership, and the power of the African lioness.

The Roaring Lioness

The lioness is an interesting specie. The continent has been blessed with them in abundance. The lioness embodies leadership that is rarely exhibited by other species in the animal kingdom. They possess a maternal instinct that is unmatched by other animals and several other qualities unique to them. Unlike other female animals, lionesses devote a significant part of their lives to mentoring and nurturing their cubs and teaching them the skills vital for their survival like hunting. To add to that they have an amazing sense of loyalty to each other and their cubs. They are the behind the scenes breadwinners in their pride who have an effective execution strategy that blends amazing teamwork and the proverbial killer instinct. Lionesses take upon themselves the responsibility to hunt for the pride, leaving the primary responsibility for the protection of the pride to the male lion.

They in many ways remind me of our very own African women, who I like to refer to as lioness leaders. The continent has been blessed with virtuous and distinguished females, who possess qualities like those of the lioness. Historically, the patriarchal systems that had become central in Africa have relegated our mothers, wives, sisters, and daughters to domestic roles and functions, however, contemporary times have seen their re-emergence to play key roles in advancing families, communities, organisations and nations.

Just as Proverbs 31:10 speaks of a virtuous woman who holds industrious and ensures that her home is well run, supplied, and catered for, we are seeing the girl child take her rightful place in Africa. Even though they are still facing resistance in certain sectors and settings owing to cultural biases and chauvinism, they are making waves nonetheless and it is time Africa embraces and celebrates them as equal partners. It is time we are more deliberate and intentional about their elevation, empowerment, and inclusion.

Since Time Immemorial

Scripture shows powerful women emerging on the continent to occupy key leadership roles that led nations in conquests and certain cases, saved nations from potential genocides. The likes of Deborah, Esther, Ruth, Rahab, the Queen of Sheba, Candace the Queen of Ethiopia, and Bathsheba as women who wielded tremendous influence in places of authority. Ancient African history testifies of powerful women who led kingdoms like Cleopatra, Nerfititi of Egypt, Queen Nandi of the Zulu Kingdom, and Queen Yaa Asantewa of the Ashanti Kingdom. Contemporary history details the exploits of women like Winnie Mandela, Sally Mugabe, Funmilayo Ransome Kuti, Vera Chirwa, Ellen Johnson Sirleaf, Folorunsho Alakija, Wendy Appelbaum and Ngina Kenyatta. The lionesses of Africa have always played a key and crucial role in leading our people in conquest politically and economically.

There are the many who oftentimes go uncelebrated but are responsible for raising generations of leaders who go on to change the world. The grandmothers who raise their grandchildren and sacrifice greatly to ensure they get an education, the sisters who fight to ensure their kinfolk get a fighting chance, the mothers who intercede tirelessly for their children, the wives who stand alongside their husbands and ensure the betterment of their legacy. The continent is blessed with this amazing and unique breed of females who are critical to God's agenda for Africa.

The Role of Women in Trade and Entrepreneurship

Our women are as gifted as our men are, and yet they do not enjoy equal access to opportunity. An example is the nation of Ghana, women are said to own more businesses than men, and yet the businesses owned by men, who are the minority, control the bulk of the economic flow. This is partly owing to the abuse and marginalisation of women when they do business. This has restricted many of our lionesses to the informal business sector, where there is a general lack of access to finance, information, and the networks that are critical to the growth and development of their businesses.

Most women on the continent are involved in cross-border trade, and with the necessary in them, be it financially, skills-wise, and through mentorship, reports suggest that we can easily add US$28 billion in GDP to the global economy by 2025. With the Africa Free Trade Agreement coming to life as well, our women are set to unleash a massive economic flow upon the economy of the Great Continent.

Making Waves Everywhere

Despite the challenge faced in many other nations as far as gender representation with regards to political participation, some African nations such as Rwanda, Tanzania, and Ethiopia have made huge strides in that regard. In some cases, we have seen women holding between 50% - 60% of leadership positions in their parliaments. This is good for the continent. It is inspiring for the future women leaders that are emerging on the continent. We need to set up systems and structures that will continually promote the recognition, empowerment, and elevation of women into a place of greater leadership.

Ruth

Scripture details the exploits of so many lionesses who redirected the destinies of nations. Deborah, Rahab, Esther, Mary the mother of Christ, to mention a few. One of my heroines in the

Bible is a woman called Ruth. She had such an incredible understanding of leadership that we all need to glean from. Ruth was a daughter-in-law of Naomi, whose husband and two sons had died in a foreign land. Both sons had married two foreign girls: Orpah and Ruth. Naomi was left alone in this country called Moab with these two daughters-in-law. She begged them to go back to their families and start new lives.

We read a very painful discussion in the book of Ruth, chapter 1 from verse 11:

And Naomi said, turn again, my daughters: why will you go with
me? Are there yet any more sons in my womb, that they may be
your husbands?
12 Turn again, my daughters, go your way; for I am too old to
have an husband. If I should say, I have hope, if I should have an
husband also tonight and should also bear sons.
13 Would you tarry for them till they were grown? Would you stay
for them from having husbands? Nay, my daughters; for it grieves
me much for your sakes that the hand of the Lord is gone out
against me.
14 And they lifted their voice and wept again: and Orpah kissed
her mother in law, but Ruth clung to her.
15 And she said, Behold, your sister-in-law is gone back to her
people, and to her gods: return you after your sister-in-law.
16 And Ruth said, Entreat me not to leave you, or return from
following after you: for where you go, I will go; and where you
lodge I will lodge: your people shall be my people and your God
shall be my God:
17 Where you die, will I die, and there will I be buried: The
Lord do so to me, and more also, if anything but death part you
and me."

Insightful Leadership

Ruth had amazing leadership insight. She realised that even though she had lost her husband and her people worshipped idols, Naomi's people were the people of God and they worshipped a living God. She was the source of Ruth's salvation now, and what she had found was larger and more important than the dead pagan husband. Even though her sister-in-law chose to go back, she was not about to be persuaded by her emotional decision, not even by the plea of her mother-in-law. Ruth was visionary enough to see the bigger picture. She had understood something that Orpah did not have the capacity for.

When we possess insight, the full understanding of something is revealed, and our attitude and behaviour are transformed. What Ruth said to her mother-in-law meant *"Please stop trying to persuade me to go back because my mind is made up. I am stuck with you; where you die, I will die."* Those are covenant words which no ordinary person can utter. Ruth had the insight into something much deeper than Naomi had ever seen. One can almost feel the tone in her voice when she said: *"Entreat me not to leave you, for where you go I will go and where you lodge I will lodge, Your people shall be my people."* Those are very strong covenant words. She is not negotiating; she has seen what she wants, she has signed the contract and is going ahead.

Generational Leadership

In today's leadership, there is a compromise in people who are supposed to be leaders. True leaders operate with a long-range vision, they make choices that are not only for now but choices that affect many generations to come. Like lionesses focus on empowering the next generation, leaders like Ruth have an eye on the future in all their actions. They appreciate that the future rests and lies on their shoulders. You must have an understanding that as a leader now, your decisions and choices will shape the future of unborn children; therefore, your decisions must be Godly.

Lionesses invest themselves in mentoring the next generation and equipping them with the skills they need to excel in the African savanna. This empowerment ensures that the cubs can perpetuate the correct legacies. Ruth went even deeper and made a statement that was so profound and so prophetic that when you read the book of Ruth with this understanding, you tremble at the weight of the statement. She said, *"Your people shall be my people and your God shall be my God."* What a statement! What truth! What Ruth was simply saying here was *"I am no longer a Moabite as you thought or as you found me; when I married your son, I took the identity of that man and we became one. Do not treat me as before. I tested and saw the God of Israel and that is the God I worship now. So, I am one with your people and I am a child of the living God, the God of Israel."*

Covenant Leadership

Ruth finally nailed it in such a way that if people were listening, they would be very surprised. She said, *"Where you die, will I die, and there will I be buried."* Here Ruth was underlining her covenant with Naomi, the people of Israel and the God of Israel. She was telling them that if they thought they could bury her in Moab, forget it! I am here to stay. Ruth spelt out her entire future for herself and for generations to come that includes us today because Ruth became a great grandmother of our Lord Jesus Christ.

I have observed this quality in so many of our African lionesses. Mothers, wives, sisters, aunts and daughters who have taken upon themselves the mantle to pray and intercede for their families – husbands, children, siblings, parents, and neighbours. This form of covenant leadership has played a key role in bringing Africa to where it is today.

Release Your ROAR

We are blessed as a continent to have this rare breed of lionesses.

CHAPTER EIGHT

STRUCTURE: ORDERING CHAOS

—∞—

"And the earth was without form, and void;
and darkness was upon the face of the deep. And the
Spirit of God moved upon the face of the waters. And God said,
"Let there be light: and there was light." And God saw the light,
that it was good: and God divided the light from the darkness.
And God called the light Day, and the darkness he called Night.
And the evening and the morning were the first day"

The book of Genesis introduces us to the creation story when God created the heavens and the earth. Verse 2 tells us of how the earth was formless and void and darkness hovered over the face of the deep. We see there a picture of chaos, pandemonium, and disorder. In response to the gloomy image that verse 2 paints in our minds, God intervened to bring order and structure to the chaos. He declares light, and light became. He called that the first day. He separates the waters to create the firmaments above and beneath. He calls that the second day. Our God proceeds to put order and structure to the world by using His word to frame it and on the sixth day, He created the first man Adam and gives him the mandate of exercising dominion in the earth, maintaining order and ensuring that the earth is as fruitful as possible. In this process, which we call the creation week, God established a system and an order that governs the earth and its operations. In the creation week, He created a predictable cycle that allows us to forecast, function, flourish, and be fruitful on earth. He created the day, the week, months, times, seasons, and cycles. This makes it possible for us to plan, organise, and exercise dominion in the earth, which is the mandate we were given as mankind.

I believe that in this Scripture we learn a lot about God, ourselves and the earth we have been given to exercise dominion over.

1. God is a God of Order and Structure.

"for God is not a God of confusion but of peace, as in all the churches of the saints"
1 Corinthians 14:33

Throughout Scripture, we see that our God is structured and orderly. We also learn that God commands a blessing wherever order exists and has been established. This is true in the human realm as it is in the spirit realm. When God led Israel out of Egypt and was building a nation out of them, He gave them to the law of Moses as an instrument for establishing order in the nation. Any people who do not have order and structure can never rise to their zenith and will not fully experience the blessing of God.

I am reminded of how we farm in the villages and on farms. Before the rains come, we till the land and we create contours and rows so that when the rain comes, we can absorb it into the ground and increase our chances for a bountiful harvest. This is a law of nature that governs the natural realm.

Africa is no exception. Just because we have an abundant flow does not guarantee an abundant harvest. Harvest is realised when and where there is order and organisation. Our continent needs us to improve our orderliness as a states, economies, and communities.

In Mark 6:40 – 44 when our Lord fed the 5000 men excluding women and children, he sat them down into groups of fifty before the disciples distributed the overflow to each person's fill. It is as though the order was a necessity and a prerequisite for the flow to be multiplied and the overflow of blessing and abundance to be experienced.

2. Human beings function best when there is order and structure.

When God created man, He set order in place before he placed the man in the garden to tend to it. In that order God commands man to be fruitful, multiply, replenish, subdue the earth and exercise dominion over it and its elements (Genesis 1:28). This order is to be established in the life of man individually, in his family, the church, community, and the nations, if man is to flourish. Here we see God's benchmark and preference for humanity. We are hardwired to thrive best when we operate under the authority and order set by the Creator.

The centurion whose servant was healed by Christ, said something of great significance when he said, *"I am a man who is under authority"* (Matthew 8:9). This principle when observed guarantees our fruitfulness and blessing in life. No kingdom or civilisation has ever excelled in the absence of order.

When Nimrod built the tower, if there was order and they all spoke with one language and understood each other, there was progress. However, the moment disorder set in, evidenced by the fact that they became incoherent and were unable to work in sync, there was destruction and chaos. This order was set by the Lord and when we live and operate within its context and confines, we assure ourselves the blessing of the Lord upon our lives and continent.

3. Order does not occur randomly.

Anything that we leave to itself will always gravitate and incline itself towards chaos and disorder. If we leave a beautiful garden unattended for a period, it is no surprise that it will find itself with weeds that can even choke the roses and obscure the beauty of the garden.

We must embrace this truth and enforce the principles of order in our nations. While we have to ensure that our constitutions are respected and the enshrined rights and freedoms for our people are protected, such liberties should never be interpreted as licences to lead lives that are reckless and defy the order set and established by God. Our systems must be respected by everyone beginning with those in authority. Corruption should never be allowed to take root in our nations. Stiff penalties must be instituted for those who violate the order we looking to create on the continent. Failing this will only lead to chaos, which will repel the blessing of God.

4. Order is the result or outcome of good leadership governance

The earth God created was already blessed with so much. Everything we see today that we define as nature or natural was already on the earth before we arrived on it. However, the earth had to be subdued if it were to serve God's purpose and mankind effectively. A few things I would like to mention here about order.

Africa needs good governance if we are going to be the prolific spring, we have the potential of becoming. The issue of Africa's abundant wealth has never been in dispute, but the absence of good governance and stewardship over the resources under our care has been the major reason for our regression and stagnation. If we are to maximise the flow and ride the rising tide, we need to put our house in order and establish improved governance on the continent. It is good that most of the continent is now democratic, but that is just a good departure point, we still need to tweak and oil our democracies for greater efficiency and more effective governance. This will allow us to grow our economies sustainably and ensure that over time we can improve the livelihoods of all our people. However, to achieve order we need sound leadership on the continent.

It needs to be clear to every despotic or rebel leader out there that the continent will not entertain any form unconstitutionalism and violation of the human rights and liberties that were attained through great sacrifice.

The Value of Good Governance

Africa has made many strides since the 1990s as far as good governance is concerned. As part of Agenda 2063, a commitment made by the African Union is to bring transformation that will see *"an Africa of good governance, democracy, respect for human rights, justice and the rule of law."* The key to Africa's political and economic transformation in the next decade is found in this aspiration. For a continent made up of so many ethnicities, social, and economic classes, we must invest in inclusive development and growth. According to the African Development Bank, good governance should be built on a foundation of:

  i. effective states,

  ii. mobilized civil societies, and

  iii. an efficient private sector.

The key elements of good governance, then, are accountability, transparency, combating corruption, citizen participation, and an enabling legal/judicial framework. Good governance is key and essential for our prosperity as a people. Our nations need constitutional reform that will redesign the governance architecture of our states ensuring a clear separation of powers and sound mechanisms for power transfer. The absence of good governance in many African countries has been extremely damaging to the government's corrective intervention role, particularly in the maintenance of peace and security, as well as the promotion of economic growth and the creation of the wealth needed to confront poverty and improve human development.

A Case for Strong Institutions

Our weak and dysfunctional governance structures continue

to prevent many African countries from creating and sustaining the necessary enabling environment for peaceful coexistence, entrepreneurship, and wealth creation. In countries such as Cameroon, the DRC, and South Sudan, the absence of sound and solid governance structures undergirded by the rule of law has been responsible for the continual failure to halt ethnic-induced violence within these states. Such failures stunt entrepreneurship and economic growth in these regions and consequently upon the whole continent. Peace and security, which are a *sine qua non* for vibrant entrepreneurial activity and the creation of wealth, are unlikely to return to these countries without the provision of participatory and inclusive governance structures.

Weak governance manifests itself in other ways as well. Dysfunctional governance processes are in place in too many of our states, creating environments where civil servants and political elites act with impunity, looting scarce public resources that could be used for education, healthcare, infrastructure, water treatment plants, electricity, farm-to-market roads, and technology. Elites are usually not inclined towards implementing pro-poor economic programs that enhance the ability of the poor to participate productively and gainfully in economic growth.

Understanding Leadership

Africa needs a new paradigm for leadership. Leadership is the ability to inspire or influence others towards a vision of a better tomorrow; it is more than management and directing. Management is about maintenance and ensuring that systems and processes are functional and on track, whereas leadership is about maximising the potential inherent in the leader, their followers, and environment. Great leaders are evidenced by the reality of the weakest or poorest among their followers. I love the Scripture that says the weakest among them shall be like David, (Zechariah 12:8), and how under Solomon's leadership silver and gold became as common as stones (2 Chronicles 1:15). Both texts testify to periods of exceptional leadership in Israel. We need such a leadership paradigm on the continent. We need leaders to be measured not by GDP figures alone, but the improvement in the quality of life index and the improvement of the livelihoods of those poorest among us.

Understanding leadership is key in everyone's life and to Africa's future. Our leaders need to embrace the reality that every human being on earth was born with leadership abilities. If we are going to pursue and develop the potential in us to its fullness, everyone needs to practice and develop our inherent leadership ability at our various levels. We must develop that ability into skill and mastery for us to become as effective as possible. It is critical to realise that inside each one of us, is a specific purpose, which is our assignment in this life and the area where we are to exercise leadership. Therefore, our leadership is driven and shaped by the calling on our individual lives; that is what distinguishes failed leadership from successful leadership. Our ability to effectively live out our individual calling and assignment.

As we develop our leadership skills, in line with our assignment – our purpose in life – it is essential to remain focused on what is expected of us as leaders at all levels. One of the biggest mistakes' leaders have made is to think that they own the people they lead. It does not work like that. Every person you lead also can lead. Great leaders develop other leaders; that is the mark of a good leader. You may lead them in one aspect of life and they also can lead you in other aspects of life.

Some presidents of countries have been voted into their positions and suddenly they think they can lead the cabinet effectively by imposing themselves on ministers and the entire nation. This kind of leadership has given birth to dictatorships and failed states. They forgot that when they were voted into power, their job was to find what the needs of the people and the country were and facilitate the development of a conducive environment for the people to be fruitful and thrive in the individual spheres of an assignment. This should be followed by them appointing men and women that have certain skills and who have a full understanding of their purposes in life. Once that stage is clear, the leaders are now properly targeted in the areas of their calling. In this setting, performance will be the target. These leaders will perform at their best always, not because they impress anyone and or doing this for money, but they are driven by what is stirring them in their hearts!

Leaders understand that their greatest assignment is to reproduce themselves by developing other leaders at every level. There should never be a leadership vacuum in government or companies. When an organization is arranged like this, there will be incredible productivity and growth.

Qualities of Effective Leaders

Effective and transformational leaders have ideas, values, energy and urgency. Ideas and values guide their decisions whilst energy and urgency fuel how a leader implements their strategies and policies. Let me break it down for your full understanding.

Ideas

Effective and successful leaders understand that ideas are capital. They appreciate that all that we see in the world today that we label as revolutionary, advanced, and progressive all began as ideas. Leaders also have clear ideas of what it takes to win in their marketplace and how their organisation should operate. They update their ideas to keep them appropriate to changing circumstances, and they help others to develop their ideas. They understand that they are responsible for setting the vision, direction, and strategy.

The Prophet Elisha was such a leader. In 2 Kings 4, a widow came to him with a major challenge, her sons were about to be taken into slavery over a debt. The prophetic leader responded with an idea that would transform her situation and turn it around. By using what she already possessed, and asking her to go and borrow as many vessels as she could, he was able to implement a revolutionary concept that saw her not only pay off her debt, but she was able to live off the overflow.

Great leaders always have ideas that unlock the flow in the favour of those they lead. Our continent needs leaders whose ideas will uplift our people, including women and youth, urban and rural, and across the entire continent of Africa.

Values

Leaders and organisations that have strong and enduring values that everyone understands and lives up to, tend to achieve greater results and outcomes than those who do not. Values guide and support ideas and when they are deeply embedded, everyone is held accountable to them, even in seemingly minor everyday decisions and actions. Exceptional leaders entrench values within the institutions and the people they lead, as this empowers all levels to make decisions that are sync with the ethos of the institution or nation.

When leaders create a system of shared values with those they lead, they release their teams to function with a greater sense of clarity and deliver superior quality results that respect and honour the guiding values of the organisations and nations they lead.

Energy

Quality leaders are not only highly energetic people, but they also actively work to create positive emotional energy in others. They do this by structuring the organisation to get rid of bureaucratic nonsense, and by stretching and encouraging everyone they meet (*extracts from The Leadership Engine by Noel M. Tichy and Eli Cohen*). Each leader goes through a phase of preparation that I want to call an *"unusual life experience."* We find different types of leaders in the Bible. The circumstances of their birth and upbringing, and their experiences, and exposures were all in preparation of how they would lead.

A classic example is that of the greatest leader Israel has ever had: King David, the man whom God called *"a man after his own heart."* In 1 Samuel 16:1, it is written, *"The Lord said to Samuel, I am sending you to Jesse of Bethlehem. I have chosen one of his sons to be king."* David was the anointed king of Israel and still went back to the bush to look after his father's sheep. One day, there was a serious battle facing the nation. The Philistines gathered their forces for war against Israel. None of the men of Israel, including their current king Saul, could challenge the leader of the Philistines' army. He was called Goliath because of his unusual stature. But the all-knowing God understood that the calling upon David, or the assignment and the anointing on David, would save the nation.

David, coming from looking after his father's sheep, had no idea that the nation was under severe threat from the Philistines. As he walked into the camp, he heard for the first time what the entire army had been told every day for two weeks. He was extremely disturbed by what he heard. In verses 26–49, we read the beautiful story on how David, full of the anointing of God, protected the nation of Israel from destruction. David had a different mindset because of the assignment on his life. Therefore, what he heard was so disturbing that he approached his brothers, asking if he could challenge Goliath. His jealous brothers wanted to chase him back to the sheep where he had come from.

David possessed the energy required and so he kept pushing until what was bothering him reached the ears of King Saul, who then permitted David to proceed after he had surrendered his leadership role to the young man David. He narrated to Saul his experiences in the bush on how he killed a bear and a lion to protect his sheep. All this was in preparation for this critical day where the future of Israel was to be determined. David was born for this; this was his time, even though none of his family members knew about him, God knew about David. None of the entire army knew about David until that day where the nation's future was to be defined. Everything gave way; the bitterness in his brothers could not stand in the way, and the hard-heartedness of Saul could not resist the anointing and the force of rare leadership skill that was on display in David's life.

Urgency

There is a sense of urgency as David began to engage with Goliath verbally. From that, we can tell that this was no ordinary fight. The outcome of this battle would not depend on man's experience. This fight was higher than any one of them; it was God's fight, and it required the one who was specially called for this. There was none but David. In his running towards the battle line, he transferred the physical battle into the spiritual realm. At this point, it was no longer David's battle; it became God's battle. David merely represented God on the battle line. In verse 45 to 47, we read that David said to the Philistine, *"You come against me with sword and spear and javelin, but I come against you in the name of the Lord Almighty, the God of the armies of Israel, whom you have defied. This day the Lord will hand you over to me, and I'll strike you down and cut off your head. Today I will give the carcasses of the Philistine army to the birds of the air and the beasts of the earth, and the whole world will know that there is a God in Israel. All those gathered here will know that it is not by sword or spear that the Lord saves; for the battle is the Lord's, and he will give all of you into our hands."*

What an amazing leader and what a rare quality of leadership!!

PART III

UNLOCKING THE FLOW

CHAPTER NINE

THE DAM EFFECT
DISRUPTING THE FLOW

—∞—

The Ethiopia Dam crisis

The River Nile represents the backbone of the early civilisations of Africa. Namely Egypt and Ethiopia. These two states were able to make huge strides in the era before Christ. A study of history will show how this territories and kingdoms were advanced in the areas of agriculture, economics, engineering, mathematics, and education. A lot of the advancements in agriculture and subsequently their economies were attributed to the massive flow of the Great River Nile. Through a study of the annual patterns of the flow of the Great River Nile, Egyptians were able to create the calendar as we have come to know it. Furthermore, they were able to harness the seasons when the Nile would overflow its banks, depositing silt that allowed their soils to experience increased and heightened fertility. This fertility gave Egypt an edge over her neighbours, as Egypt would enjoy relative abundance even in famine when contrasted to the other kingdoms around her. It is therefore no surprise that when Abraham experienced famine in his day, he migrated down to Africa for about seven years. When drought struck in Isaac's time, he was about to come down to Egypt as well, till the Lord told him to dwell in Gerar. Jacob also migrated to Egypt when the famine became extremely sore and lack had overwhelmed him. The Lord had sent Joseph to Egypt because it had a flow that Joseph had the wisdom and grace to manage and maximise, so he could save many alive.

The Power of a Flow

It is amazing how a flow can become the backbone of a civilisation and a great nation. It therefore makes sense why Africa has always been at the centre of so many conflicts. When we consider nations like the Democratic Republic of the Congo and South Sudan, which have not known stability in a while, we realise that beneath the ethnic tensions is a battle to control the flow in favour of one group versus another. Now, allow me a rabbit trail here, if we were aware of the abundance of wealth under our feet, we would be wiser to join hands, forces, minds, skills, capital, and resources so we can maximise what we have been blessed with, instead of being divided and destructive because we refuse to collaborate and share the gains. There is more than enough wealth in our nations to serve every single one of us and our posterity for generations to come.

Ethiopia and Egypt

One conflict I would like us to zero in on, is Ethiopia, Sudan, and Egypt Blue Nile crisis. In her development plans Ethiopia sought to electrify its communities and its surrounding nations by building The Grand Ethiopia Renaissance Dam on the Nile. The dam would allow them to capture the flow and channel it towards power generation which will allow it to increase access of electricity to the more 65% of their population that is not connected to their national grid. Egypt on the other hand is arguing that this presents a huge risk to them as 90% of its fresh water supply comes from the Nile. This would also affect Egypt's agricultural industry negatively and their economy as a result. To bridge the disparity existing between the three nations on this issue, dialogue has been pursued but an agreement is yet to be reached. The debate is not centred around Ethiopia's development plans, but around how the dam affects the flow and rearranges the balance of power in the region.

Egypt is arguing that the dam should be filled at a much slower rate than Ethiopia is proposing, and that in times of drought Ethiopia must allow the flow to reach Egypt so that it can fill up its main dam and sustain its activities. Ethiopia on the other hand is looking to accelerate their development agenda, they are arguing that the flow originates from lakes within their territory and as such they would like to fill up the dam within four to seven years as opposed to Egypt proposal of filling the dam in twenty years. The deadlock relates to who will control the flow. Whoever has greater control of the flow, can derive maximum benefit for their economy. Sudan is caught in the middle, they stand to benefit from cheaper hydroelectric power for their own developmental needs, but their concern relates to the geopolitical impact this would have on the region, as the dam will dramatically shift the balance of power in Ethiopia's favour.

It is also interesting to note that 86% of the natural flow of this river emanates from Ethiopia, but the benefit that Ethiopia has derived from the flow has been minimal. This has been traced back to the 1929 Nile Waters Agreement which gave Egypt veto power over any projects on the Nile. In another 1959 agreement between Egypt and Sudan, in which Ethiopia was never consulted, Egypt was granted most of the Nile waters and Sudan was apportioned a sizeable allocation.

Interestingly, the Ethiopian scenario mirrors the African reality too much to be ignored. Firstly, the flow of the Nile emanates mostly from Ethiopia, but very little benefit has been realised by Ethiopia. Secondly, the deals were negotiated and cut without the source itself being considered or consulted. Thirdly, the moment Ethiopia decides to harness its flows towards its own developmental agenda, a crisis with Egypt, who have been monopolising the gains of the flow, suddenly erupts. Egypt is essentially insisting that Ethiopia is free to build its dam, but they must not disrupt the flow. This sounds all too familiar doesn't it? I do hope and pray that as you are reading this book, whenever that maybe, this crisis that is now being mediated by the African Union would have found resolution, to common good of not only the three nations, but for Africa as a whole.

The Power of Dams

The challenge that we will always encounter with most flows, principally rivers, is that they are in constant motion as they journey from source to mouth. This simply means they are migratory by nature, and their benefit may not be fully realised until they are captured and harnessed. One way we can do that is by building dams along an existing flow. This allows us to collect as much of the flow as practically possible and channel it towards the development and improvement of the communities, economies, and livelihoods around its flow. In the case of Ethiopia, the dam they are constructing allows them to harness the flow of the Nile and redirect towards their economic development agenda.

A dam allows us to optimise the value of the river and its flow and entire economies and civilisations can be built around the captured flow, and downstream opportunities can be created as a result. This is the kind of thinking that we need to adopt as a continent, not only around the flows of our rivers, but those of our wealth and industries. If for example, we have an agricultural estate in a community that is growing tea, cocoa, or coffee for export, instead of simply putting up an airstrip or road infrastructure to get the produce to market in its freshest state, we should be about creating a dam effect, that will allow optimal benefit to be derived by the local community and economy. We could for example set up community banks where a predefined percentage of export proceeds must be invested by the exporting farmers for lending to support local enterprise development, a research and development institute that will train locals to improve the quality of the produce grown in the area, or an international market where international buyers come and bid so that maximum pricing is achieved. We could even explore schemes that will allow small scale farmers to benefit from contracts offered by the transnational entity to grow the same produce which will be admitted into the same export markets and see these communities earn much needed foreign currency, which can be applied towards the development of local infrastructure.

Africa's Diamond Industry: A Case in Point

It appears our nations, economies, and communities suffer greatly from a similar catch twenty-two scenario. Whenever we determine to harness our resources to benefit our people and continent, deadlocks emerge. The issue between Egypt, Ethiopia and Sudan is one of control. If dams are built upstream first, they allow the flow to be harnessed and channelled to benefit those around the source of the flow before it can then benefit those who are downstream. Of the top ten diamond producing nations in the world ten are in Africa. According to the World Diamond Council, Africa produces over 65% of global output. However, when one analyses the global diamond industry, very little of the value addition is done on the continent. India, which is not even a top ten producer, hosts the world's largest diamond polishing and cutting industry, and employs over 700,000 workers in Surat, a city which accounts for just about half of the exports of diamonds from India, and yet Africa only employs a paltry 38,000 people.

Imagine with me for second, what would happen if Africa's top ten diamond producing nations decided to industrialise around the source. How many jobs we could create, how much skilling we could achieve for our people, and just how much value we could capture and channel into the very communities that God blessed with the resource. I am not just speaking of our nations, but the unelectrified and poorly developed rural communities around our mines. This would upset the status quo and disrupt the current equilibrium that is keeping our people in constant struggle and poverty. It would undoubtedly turn the tide in our favour.

Creating Special Economic Zones

The diamond industry is a simple case in point, but one that reflects what we can do across various industries, especially with the Africa Free Trade Agreement going live in 2021. We can do this with manufacturing, whereby regional blocs can create a favourable investment climate that offers tax incentives, relaxed exchange control restrictions, and other incentives for the stimulation of investment into the regions. These zones can be created around key resources and/or areas that need to experience rapid economic growth as a means of alleviating the developmental challenges around us. The regional nature of these zones will allow for greater synergies to be built and that will improve competitiveness and quality of products and services created in the zones. These zones can focus on agro-based manufacturing, hospitality and tourism, mineral beneficiation, technological advancement, aquaculture and many other industries that we can harness.

Devolution: Creating Shared Prosperity

If we are going to effectively harness the dam effect on the continent one of the challenges Africa needs to deal with is the centralisation of government and economic activity in capital cities and urban areas, and allow provincial and local governments to develop their own policies and incentives that will attract investment and allow for accelerated development on a broad based level. In Africa, it is generally believed that devolution is the panacea to the incessant infrastructure backlogs, poor service delivery, inequalities, high rates of unemployment at the grassroots and the high household poverty rates. The general belief is that the provincial and local tiers of government are critical in mitigating the effects of the challenges that have affected the generality of citizens. Devolution thus entails the reconstruction of communities, the environment and the bedrock of a democratic, integrated, prosperous and unified nation-state.

Devolution will allow economic revival and stimulation to begin at a very grassroots level and will allow the benefits of the flow to be shared amongst more people beginning with those closest to our sources of wealth; the mines, farms, conservancies, lakes etc. As lower levels of government are empowered to have the ability to co-ordinate, monitor, and attract investment activities within their locales, we can dramatically improve our ability to achieve broad based empowerment for our locals. Ethiopia's example is truly a game changer, one we must adopt in all nations, industries, and sectors. We simply need to be bold and courageous as Joshua was, and act decisively and responsibly, and our posterity will be grateful for the sacrifice we make on their behalf. The tide is rising, and we need to rise to the occasion and step up to the plate. *Ke nako, kairos* is here.

CHAPTER TEN

STEWARDSHIP

—∞—

"For unto whomsoever much is given, of him shall be much required: and to whom men have committed much, of him they will ask the more.
Luke 12:48

The law of faithfulness and stewardship is a revolutionary concept instituted by the Lord. It has the power to radically transform the lives of those who live and operate by it. It teaches us about the Kingdom of Heaven and at the same time gives us Divine principles to live by here on earth. From it, we understand that whenever God has blessed a person or a people with something of worth and value, He has an expectation that is in sync with the measure and the degree of the blessing bestowed. When one has been given little, it is only fair to demand a return that is commensurate with what has been bestowed. The opposite is equally true when one has been entrusted with much, they are also expected to yield a return that is in line with what they have been given. This should cause our hearts as Africans to skip a beat for a second or two, because of all the continents of the earth none has been as blessed as we are. We have never been a cursed people or continent. We are blessed with so much abundance of wealth and resource. The issue that should preoccupy our minds as Africa and Africans, is not one of blessing or curse, but one of stewardship.

Stewardship Defined

A steward is one who has been entrusted to take care of that which belongs to another. We all know that the earth is the Lord's and the fullness thereof, this includes the Great Continent of Africa, it belongs to none of us, it is His and His alone (Psalms 24:1). We are simply stewards entrusted to manage it faithfully so that we can pass it on to future generations who must follow suit and exercise even greater stewardship over it. Scripture teaches us that there is an expectation that stewards are to be found faithful (2 Corinthians 4:4.) Faithfulness does not mean maintaining what has been given to our trust in the same state that it has been given to us. No, the Bible defines such behaviour as wickedness and slothfulness. Faithfulness transcends maintenance and management; it is about increasing the value of the master's goods and the benefit He reaps from his investment. As people blessed with such a beautiful and amazing continent, we are to take what we have been given and work diligently to improve its condition, increase its value, multiply it for His glory and honour and ensure that the Master receives greater return on His investment. This is the mandate upon us as the children of God who were placed on the continent for such a time as this.

We are being called to faithful stewardship over what we have now. You could be running a small agricultural garden in your backyard or on a plot in your village, you must commit yourself to be faithful in that regard. You are to work diligently to improve your yields both in quality and quantity. You might be a teacher who is raising the next generation of thinkers and leaders, God has made you a steward over those amazing leaders of tomorrow, pour into them more than what your remuneration and job description demand. Remember your faithfulness is not towards man, but towards God who gave you that mandate and job as a steward of His grace and gifts Raise students who will become innovators that will solve the challenges that confront us as a people, maybe one day you will be elevated to the level of a policymaker who will make a difference on a much larger scale. Remember that to him who is faithful with little, God will make them a ruler over much (Luke 16:10).

Principles of Stewardship

Matthew 25: 14 -30 is one of the most descriptive parables that deal with faithfulness and how our God honours it. There are a few principles that I would like to extract from this and other key texts that will help and empower every African to rise and operate in an increase of the flow that has been entrusted to them. This is not restricted to our individual lives but pertains to our work lives, business, governments, churches and nations. A nation that is unfaithful with the resources under its steward-ship, will never be able to experience an increase in its flow. This is a principle that rings true regardless of whether they are Christian or not. When people are good stewards of anything, they at-tract the blessing of God that brings with it an evident and unde-niable increase.

"For the kingdom of heaven is as a man travelling into a far country, who called his own servants, and delivered unto them his goods.

And unto one he gave five talents, to another two, and to another one; to every man according to his several ability; and straightway took his journey.

Then he that had received the five talents went and traded with the same and made them other five talents.

And likewise, he that had received two, he also gained other two.

But he that had received one went and digged in the earth and hid his lord's money.

After a long time, the lord of those servants cometh, and reck-oneth with them.

And so, he that had received five talents came and brought other five talents, saying, Lord, thou deliveredst unto me five talents:

behold, I have gained beside them five talents more. His lord said unto him, Well done, thou good and faithful servant: thou hast been faithful over a few things, I will make thee ruler over many things: enter thou into the joy of thy lord.

He also that had received two talents came and said, Lord, thou deliveredst unto me two talents: behold, I have gained two other talents beside them.

His lord said unto him, Well done, good and faithful servant; thou hast been faithful over a few things, I will make thee ruler over many things: enter thou into the joy of thy lord.

Then he which had received the one talent came and said, Lord, I knew thee that thou art an hard man, reaping where thou hast not sown, and gathering where thou hast not strawed:

And I was afraid and went and hid thy talent in the earth: lo, there thou hast that is thine.

His lord answered and said unto him, Thou wicked and slothful servant, thou knewest that I reap where I sowed not, and gather where I have not strawed:

Thou oughtest therefore to have put my money to the exchangers, and then at my coming I should have received mine own with usury.

Take therefore the talent from him and give it unto him which hath ten talents.

For unto everyone that hath shall be given, and he shall have abundance: but from him, that hath not shall be taken away even that which he hath.

And cast ye the unprofitable servant into outer darkness: there shall be weeping and gnashing of teeth."

Principle #1: God Owns Everything

v 14 "For the kingdom of heaven is as a man travelling into a far country, who called his own servants, and delivered unto them his goods."

Scripture is very clear who owns the earth and everything therein, God and God alone. From the minerals under our feet, the wildlife in our game reserves, the human beings in our populations, to the land, which we have divided amongst ourselves and have given title to each other as security, they are all God's. We are at best stewards who have been entrusted with that which belongs to our Creator. Africa needs to appreciate this truth, and this should cause us much fear and trembling to arrest us regardless of who we are.

No government, private enterprise, or individual owns anything in this earth. We must therefore take time to ask ourselves what the owner expects of us as his servants and stewards who he has over his property.

Principle#2: God Entrusts Us According to Our Ability
v 15 "And unto one he gave five talents, to another two, and to another one; to every man according to his several ability; and straightway took his journey."
God blesses people and nations according to His investment of ability in them. Selah! The fact that our continent has been entrusted to be the fountain of global wealth should tell us something unique and special about us as a people and the abilities and capacity we have. God would never dump his best resources in the hands of slothful and incapable people. It is not in His nature to entrust all this gold, oil, gas, wildlife, arable land, a young and resourceful population to us if we did not possess the capacity to faithfully steward over it all to His glory.

Africa, you are capable of being faithful stewards who can effectively manage this abundant flow and serve the needs of humanity.

Principle #3: God Gives Us Time to Prove Our Stewardship and Faithfulness
v 19 After a long time the lord of those servants cometh, and reckoneth with them.
Our God is not only good and amazing, He is also fair and just. He not only gave us an incredible continent to serve as stew-

ards over, He has also given us time to work to achieve results according to His investment and expectation. We are to be faithful stewards not only over the resources we have been entrusted with, but we are to be faithful with our time. Our failure to manage time appropriately will cost us an increase in the flow we have.

There is no need for us to be in a rush to the point where we become clumsy and unproductive. We should take the time to plan, structure, strategise and execute with the excellence that we need to be globally competitive. We need to be patient with ourselves without losing that much-needed sense of urgency. Every day, hour, minute and second of time must count for something productive.

If we take time to study nations that have been able to increase the flow within their economies, we see that they are productive with their time. They have an appreciation of its value and understand that time lost can never be regained. May God give us the grace to be exceptional stewards over the time he has given to us.

Principle #4: We Have to Trade Diligently in the Marketplace with what is Under Our Stewardship

v 16 Then he that had received the five talents went and traded with the same and made them other five talents.

God never blessed people so they can hoard what they have been entrusted with. The spring is to be a blessing that will water the nations. Imagine with me for a second, if you were locked up in the vault where China, which has the world's largest reserves of foreign currency, would you be happy knowing you had all that money at your disposal but you could not trade with anyone because no one wanted or needed it? I am sure you would not be. Whatever you have can only be considered valuable if someone was willing to exchange equal value for it, because the power is in trade.

For decades Africa was receiving huge inflows of aid, which we have come refer to as dead aid. This era crippled Africa significantly because it stopped our people from being productive with our God-given resources and trading. However, the tide is turning now, we are learning that increase comes not from receiving but from learning to grow what we have so we can trade with other continents and as result, our economies have been growing, the inflows into our continent have been increasing and we have been able to grow economically. We have been creating jobs, businesses, and our incomes and exports have been rising because the key lies in trade and not in aid.

Principle #5: Stewardship Is About Creating Return on The Lord's Investment

God blessed Africa with an abundance of raw materials. These were given to us so we can harness them to the betterment of our lives, livelihoods, and continent. Our failure to add value to these is bad stewardship. When we export raw materials and import finished goods, we are being wicked and slothful like the one who was given one talent and brought the same back to the Master.

Is this not what we are doing? Extracting crude oil in the Delta, Angola, and Equatorial Guinea, and yet till this day, we do not have an African conglomerate that refines oil for domestic use? My fellow African brothers and sister, such wicked and slothful stewardship is costing us dearly. Therefore, we keep losing more and more of our flow to those who are being more diligent about adding value before trading than we are. Thank God, the narrative is changing.

Principle #6: We Are to Give an Account of Our Stewardship

With stewardship comes accountability. As we mentioned in the first principle, God is the owner of all things, and such we shall have to account to him regarding our stewardship not to man but God. This is a paradigm-shifting truth, one which radically alters our attitude towards our continent. Imagine if politicians, chiefs, business leaders, investors, civil society, judicial officers, civil servants, health care professionals, childminders, street cleaners, farmers, market vendors, and every one of us adopted this mindset, what sort of revolution would we see on the continent? We would experience a boom of such epic proportions that the world will come to Africa with notebooks and pens and ask us, "How did you do it?" Our response will be, "We learnt that we are accountable to God first."

In our accountability, God will be looking to see how we have created value and multiplied what He left under our trust. Did we improve the infrastructure we inherited from previous generations? Did we create more jobs than what previous administrations did? Were you able to open new markets for local exports? Were you able to increase the quality of our graduates? Did we create a more conducive environment for SMME's to thrive? Did we do all in our power to educate that child with special needs? Ask yourself today and amend your ways, because one day you and I shall account not before a parliamentary committee, or a judicial commission, but before the One whose eyes see deeper than our sweet words?

Principle #7: Good Stewardship Leads to Abundance

v 20 And so he that had received five talents came and brought other five talents, saying, Lord, thou deliveredst unto me five talents: behold, I have gained beside them five talents more.
v 21 His lord said unto him, Well done, good and faithful servant; thou hast been faithful over a few things, I will make thee ruler over many things: enter thou into the joy of thy lord.

The servants who demonstrated good stewardship were rewarded with an increase and the one who did not show good stewardship was not. What he had was taken away from him and given to the one who had been a good steward, so that he could continue to increase the Master's investment. I pray that as Africa we come to master the concept and discipline of good stewardship across all our communities, economies, and nations. My heartfelt desire is to see our loving God reward us for good stewardship. I believe that this is one of the ways we are going to leapfrog ourselves from the place we find ourselves to the one we are destined to occupy. When we are faithful with little; the small plot, the corner store, the table in the flea market, the business operating from our small home office, or the small-scale artisanal mine; God rewards us by shifting us into greater abundance. Promotion should not be permission to lose commitment to good stewardship. We must maintain the discipline so that God rewards our continent with more abundance so that the quality of our people's livelihoods may continue to improve.

A Call to Business Leaders

I have been in business for over three decades now. I remember when I started, I had a dream and I saw possibility. I did not have much to invest besides my time and energy, so I gave myself faithfully in that regard. I had to appreciate that I was not in this business for money, but it was my heartfelt service to God as I faithfully served him with my gift. Instead of adopting the mentality of a squanderer, I chose to be a faithful steward who invests back into the business and allows it to grow so that God is glorified by the work of my hands. I am glad to say to the glory of God that the business I started many years ago, I have passed the reins on to my son Tinashe, he is now the CEO. I am still involved but as the Chairman, for this is part of the seamless succession we are looking to implement. I knew from day one that this business was never mine. It has always and will always belong to God. My responsibility has been to serve as a faithful steward over it. The new CEO is aware of this too. He knows that he is not in that position because he is my son, he is in that position because he has served faithfully as steward from the day, he joined the business. In the ethos of the organisation we do not reward slothfulness, we reward faithfulness, one's ability to grow what has been given under their care. This is how any business can perpetuate itself when we raise leaders because of their faithfulness and not because of our relationship.

My son Tinashe has been able to take the business to levels beyond my imagination. Under his stewardship and leadership, the organisation has grown, he has been able to improve our technological capacity as a company, our staff complement has grown in quality and quantity. It is my prayer that more than making me proud, that he makes his Heavenly Father proud.

My challenge to my fellow brothers and sisters who are in business on the continent is let us be faithful stewards on the continent. Let us manage the continent's resources in a manner that glorifies God. Let us be about our Father's business with diligence and let us nor be slothful in any way. Let us faithfully administer what is under our care and ensure that we do not rob our communities but instead let us empower them so that together we can faithfully serve as stewards over the continent.

A Call to Government Leaders

Government leaders are servants and stewards of the Most High. This means one day they shall be held accountable before the Master. I challenge our leaders at all levels of government, from Heads of States down to those who serve at the grassroots levels within our communities, cabinet ministers, Directors of government departments, senators, members of parliament and houses of assembly, and our councillors, to be faithful as stewards entrusted by God to serve Him and His people faithfully.

Africa needs you to be diligent in service. The culture of corruption, nepotism, tribalism, and petty politics must be done away with forthwith. We need leaders whose heart is to serve all from the least to the greatest. We need you to return to the principles of servant leadership, where you appreciate that he that desires to be the leader must first become a servant. You are called to be good stewards over the people and resources under your trust.

Politics and government should never be get-rich quick schemes. You exist to serve and so I challenge you to serve with excellence and take good care of the continent for it is the Lord's.

A Call to Church Leaders

One of the greatest pillars that we have on the continent is the Body of Christ. Africa can never walk into her prophetic destiny without the people of God playing the crucial role assigned to them. When we humble ourselves and pray and turn from our wicked ways, God will hear us and heal our continent. We need to unite and seek the face of God on behalf of our continent. We need to take our place as intercessors and priests who stand in the gap for the land that God may bring us into our own.

We are to raise God-fearing leaders within our communities, we are to challenge our members to be faithful in their roles at work, as entrepreneurs, doctors, maids, drivers, technocrats, artists, teachers, nurses, civil servants etc. We are to culture our people to have the kind of work ethic that glorifies God.

CHAPTER ELEVEN

SHREWD AS SERPENTS

—⚮—

"The serpent was the shrewdest of all the wild animals the LORD God had made."
Genesis 3:1

When our Lord commissioned His disciples as He sent them out on their mission, He reminded them that they were being sent as sheep among wolves. His commandment to them was that they were to be as shrewd as serpents and be humble as doves. The metaphors at play here are quite revelatory.

Firstly, we have wolves. Wolves are ravenous predators. They are cunning, calculating, and ruthless bloodthirsty creatures. They have the patience that can deceive you into thinking they mean no harm, only to wait for that moment when your guard is down and strike swiftly. Wolves have loyalties only to their bellies and voracious appetites. They are also cunning enough to blend in with the sheep, only to strike with lethal force when least expected. Wolves are masters of disguise and can fool you by how they present themselves. The phrase, wolves in sheep's clothing, is not just cliché, it is revealing of the character and nature of these marauding beasts.

Secondly, we have sheep. Sheep are generally gentle, innocent, simple, unassuming, and undiscerning. They are the perfect prey for the subtle wolf. Sheep are not only desirable for their fresh and juicy flesh, but their simple-mindedness also makes the task of the wily predatorial wolves much simpler. In simplicity and total dependence of their shepherd to do all the thinking for them, sheep hardly ever think or project beyond their immediate environment and as such, they are very susceptible to becoming victims of an unsuspected strike from the wolves. They follow blindly and never question themselves or the one wooing them, even if it is to the slaughter.

Thirdly, our Lord gives us the metaphor of the serpent. A creature which many of have an uneasy relationship. Our Lord is however challenging us to appreciate the importance of this reptile character and nature in navigating this predatorial reality. The environment we are operating in requires us, those who are as sheep among wolves, to be as wise as serpents in our dealings. Meaning there is something about this venomous creature we must learn and adapt in our interactions. Serpents are extremely sensitive beings. They are very careful and cautious, extremely discerning, stealth, and generally operate with a high level of mistrust. The weakness of the serpent is its propensity to strike at even the most innocent of intruders of its environment. To the serpent, there are no innocent guests.

The fourth metaphor is that of a dove. We are being instructed that to operate in this cutthroat world, we must learn the shrewdness of the serpent and be as harmless as doves. Doves are gentle. They are as sensitive to threats as the serpent, but they differ in response and reaction to a perceived threat. Where the serpent strikes, the dove withdraws.

Lessons from the Metaphors
1. We Operate in Predatorial World

The Lord is reminding us here of the nature of the landscape that we are operating in. A continent as richly blessed as the one we have been made stewards over, will without fail, attract wolves. As we mentioned above, these are ruthless predatorial creatures who are in the game for the kill. It would be folly of us to deal, interact, and negotiate with these pillaging and marauding beings with no discretion. The simplicity of thought and the innocence of naivety that are typical of sheep must be done away with. The stakes we face are too high for us to be un-calculating and scrupulous as we navigate this dog eat dog world.

The global economy is an imperialistic and capitalist terrain, run on the principle of the survival of the fittest. It is a cutthroat world. It is a kill or get killed space. This should never shock us. Consider the wars and conflicts that have characterised the continent over the past few centuries. They attest to the nature of the world we live in. These conflicts are generally driven by the greed of predatorial elements and ravenous interests who are in it only for what is in it for them.

2. We Are Sheep by Nature

In being challenged to appreciate the reality of the landscape we find ourselves in, is not a call to change who we are. As sons and daughters of the Most High we do not need to alter our Christ nature and character for us to survive and thrive in this kind of environment. We do not need to think and function like the marauding and pillaging wolves. There is no need for us to become cunning, deceptive, and dishonourable. We must never demean ourselves and our Creator by choosing to operate as such a low altitude. We are sheep by nature because we follow our Good Shepherd, and our sheep hearts keep us sensitive to His voice so that we do not follow the voice of a stranger. We must never change our nature for the sake of silver and gold. But that does not mean we must remain naïve and unassuming. The environment demands that we develop sensitivities and capabilities that are not common among sheep.

3. The Level Playing Field is Tilted Against Us

The Scripture also tacitly reminds us of a cold fact, one which I believe relates to the African and Christian context well. The landscape does not favour us at all. Like sheep, we are the weak, inexperienced, and defenceless. The wolves on the other hand are the strong, dominant, and ruthless ones. If we were to engage with the world of global capital as sheep taking on wolves, we do not stand a chance at turning the tide in our favour. New approaches, attitudes, and ways of doing business need to be adopted. Thank God, our Lord has equipped us with the wisdom to do exactly that.

4. We Are to Operate with the Shrewdness of Serpents

The challenge to be as shrewd as serpents is a call to adaptation to the environment without compromising our core biblical values. Our sheep nature speaks to our hearts, which are to always remain kind-hearted, well-meaning, and innocent. Our minds, however, are not to be naïve.

Remember how Esau's naivety cost him his birth right, and he lost to his cunning and supplanting brother Jacob? We as Africans cannot afford to continually deal with the world as a gullible people. We are to develop shrewdness of mind. As African leaders in business, government, the church and in our communities, we need to be adept in all our dealings, if we are going to benefit from the magnanimous tide that is rising. The rising tide will attract wolves and we cannot afford to engage with them as sheep as we have done in history.

5. We Are to Respond with the Gentleness of Doves

Doves are known for their sensitivity to any given environment they find themselves in. Doves are so innocent that they do not harm anyone or any creature. Likewise, when we deal with the predatory elements who desire access to our resources and markets, we should marry the shrewdness of the serpent with the gentleness of the dove. Once we have discerned the malintent of these players, instead of responding like serpents, or sheep, we are to respond with the gentle diplomacy of doves. Responding with a serpentine approach, which normally is striking lethally, will have grave consequences on us and our future. Remember, we are still sheep, only that we have learnt to operate as serpents and doves.

6. The Landscape Does Not Favour Us but We Can Adapt to Our Favour

Africa has only one way to survive and thrive in this global jungle. We must adapt and develop mastery in the areas that we are weak in. Our sheepish nature as I have mentioned earlier predisposes us to vulnerability. However, when we learn to operate like serpents and doves, we can adapt to this stubborn landscape that does not favour us and thrive in it.

We must be shrewd when we deal with those who come from both East and West bearing gifts. We must be careful of those who many times seek to corrupt our leaders so they can gain access and control of our extractive industries and key markets. These are many times wolves, who are simply out to sink their carnivorous teeth into our economies and drain the flow, leaving us destitute and barren.

It is only when we adapt without compromising who we are and what we stand for, that we stand a chance to win. We must stand for ownership of the resources by our people and the communities that God has blessed with them. We need to stand firm on issues of employment of locals, the support of downstream and upstream businesses in the local economy, and the investment into improving local infrastructure before any investment is welcome. We must be shrewd as serpents, we must be territorial about our resources, and guard them as a serpent guards its space. We must also remember the diplomacy of the dove and extend an olive branch while defending our interests.

What Has This Got to Do with the Flow

"But the sons of Israel were fruitful and] increased greatly, and multiplied, and became exceedingly mighty so that the land was filled with them. Now a new king arose over Egypt, who did not know Joseph. And he said to his people, "Behold, the people of the sons of Israel are] too many and too mighty for us. Come, let us deal shrewdly with them, otherwise they will multiply, and in the event of war, they will also join those who hate us, and fight against us and depart from the land." So, they appointed task-masters over them to oppress them with] hard labour. And they built for Pharaoh storage cities, Pithom and Raamses. But the more they oppressed them, the more they multiplied and the more they spread out, so that they dreaded the sons of Israel."

Exodus 1:7-12

The global economic landscape is one where the tactical advantage belongs to the one who possesses a higher degree of shrewdness. The playing field is tilted in the favour of the perceptive and judicious. Shrewdness carries so much power and potency that it can turn any disadvantage into favour. When one is shrewd, they demonstrate a knack that transcends power, talent, and numbers. Prudence makes an individual capable of achieving the seemingly impossible, as we will observe in this chapter.

When a Pharaoh emerged in Egypt who did not know Joseph, he identified the children of Israel as a threat to his agenda. God had blessed the household of Israel, who had migrated into Egypt as a group of seventy-five individuals, and He had made them a nation. They had multiplied greatly and had become exceedingly mighty as a people. The balance of power in Egypt gave Pharaoh the chills. He cited how their numbers and collective strength made them a significant force and thus an imminent threat to his agenda. Pharaoh needed to subjugate Israel and use her might and numbers for his development agenda for Egypt.

Pharaoh knew fully well that he could never overpower and succeed. They were more and mightier. Pharaoh had no illusions about that, so he sought a more effective way of turning the balance of power and wealth in the favour of Egypt. He chose to deal wisely and shrewdly with Israel. By dealing with them prudentially he was able to turn the powerful Israelites into a slave nation.

Africa in Context

Sadly, the case of Israel and Egypt mirrors that of Africa and the developed world. Firstly, like Israel, we have the numbers and wealth. We are a majority with no authority in the global environment. There is no logical explanation for our weak state, except to say our advantages have been subtly taken from us.

Secondly, like Israel, our destiny has been and is being discussed in places we are not invited to participate in. Africa is truly on the dinner table and her wealth are being dished out to the embellishment of those who have no deep connection to her.

Thirdly, a shrewd plan and system has been and is being engineered to overturn our advantage into a disadvantage by strategically and systematically weakening us as a people. This is happening in both Eastern and Western nations. Everybody wants to weaken the African so they can continually rape the continent of her resources, while her narrative of poverty continues.

Shrewdness: A Must-Have Competence

Africa is an oxymoron and a paradox because we have not exercised shrewdness and discernment in our dealings and transactions over the centuries. We have negotiated treaties that have far-reaching implications, with thoughtless naivety. We lost our upper hand, not because of our weakness or lack of power or wealth, but because we were hasty and imprudent in negotiation. Our forefathers traded wealth laden lands in exchange for arms that would soon be obsolete and for no value. Sadly, our contemporary leaders, some of whom have matriculated from the world's prime institutes of learning, are repeating the same folly and inept behaviour, giving away diamonds mines in exchange for AK47's and luxury villas. In the absence of farsighted and calculated thinking, Africa will be dealt with shrewdly by crafty and cunning business leaders who have one agenda, subjugating the continent for their agendas.

Simple Mindedness is High-Risk Attitude

As you recall in earlier chapters, we looked at the ongoing scramble for Africa's flow of resources, her trade routes, human capital, and consumer markets. This scramble is real my brothers and sisters. African leaders are constantly being serenaded by investors from all over the globe. Many of these investors can be likened to the wolves described above and our continent; its people, governments, and markets can be likened to the sheep. We are generally viewed as unsuspecting, naïve and simple-minded people who for whatever reason believe that everyone in the world loves us and wants what is best for us including these bloodthirsty wolves.

We must embrace the facts of the terrain if we are going to successfully turn the tide in Africa's favour. The global business environment is populated by ravenous wolves. They scout the continent in search of vulnerable nations, naïve businesspeople, and simple-minded communities and government leaders, who they can deceive and lure so they can make dinner of them. These wolves are not here for trade, neither are they in this for win/win deals. Their mission is consistent with their predatory nature, they are looking for a kill and they are not here to take prisoners either.

As a continent that only managed to successfully liberate itself a little over a quarter of a century ago, many of our politicians and indigenous business leaders are relatively new to the game of dealing with the predatorial international investment community. Sadly, many transactions that pertain to our massive flows are negotiated by sheeply leaders whose eagerness to create jobs and deliver on ambitious and inflated electoral promises exposes them to the many unscrupulous investors who see Africa as a get rich quick scheme. These investors thrive in environments where governments are financially desperate and isolated from the community of nations with weak state institutions and a stifled civil society. These predatory corporations are not merely bystanders conducting business as usual in an unsavoury environment. They often are known to proactively empower unaccountable leaders and frequently benefit directly from conflict and political crises. These companies can make a fortune from resource-rich fragile states. Such nations are the primary prey of these marauders.

The predatory investors that have been sucking Africa's flows for a song often serve the short-term interests of senior officials and do not benefit the citizens much. Billions of dollars' worth of resources are extracted annually from the soil of the nations involved but the living standards of our people never improve noticeably.

Wiser in their Time

"The master praised the unrighteous manager because he had acted shrewdly. For the children of this age are more shrewd than the children of light in dealing with their own people."

Luke 16:8

A wise man is one who takes time to understand a landscape and its intricacies and adapt to it. Shrewd individuals are those who are analytical, critical, calculative, and wily in their thinking. They are those who Ecclesiastes refers to as having eyes in their heads (Ecclesiastes 2:14). The level of shrewdness that a person or a people possess determines how much of the flow they get to benefit from. Africa as the fountain and steward of God's resources on the continent has for many centuries suffered from many social and economic ills not because we are cursed, but because we have not been wise in dealing with the rest of the world.

The parable of the unjust and dishonest steward reveals to us how one can transform their fate by dealing wisely. The Lord commends the children of this world by affirming their ability to deal with their own kind in a foxy way. They appreciate that they are dealing with wolves and as such, they adapt and deal with their own accordingly. The unjust steward understood the thinking inherent in his master's debtors. He knew that they would take a deal that would lighten their debt burden any day, so he proceeded to make them offers that they could not turn down. In so doing, he not only was able to earn a living, but he was also able to win the hearts of the very same debtors.

Shrewd and calculative people are needed more than ever at all levels and in all sectors of African life. The continent needs to invest in creating, mentoring, coaching, and training such leaders now more than ever. We need them in all sectors of the economy, in education, healthcare, social services, and the pulpit as well. These are the kinds of individuals who can start businesses with little to no capital because they understand how to leverage their advantage even when to the naked eye, they may appear disadvantaged. Thank God we have judicious leaders emerging on the continent, but we need more of them to rise so we can effectively change the flow to our favour.

CHAPTER TWELVE

THE POWER OF STRATEGY
MAXIMISING THE FLOW

—⚮—

After God had given Abraham the prophetic promise that his descendants would one day be slaves in a foreign land, it was inconceivable to have imagined how that was going to play out. God would allow Joseph, a young man, with exceptional qualities to be sold by his brethren into slavery. The Ishmaelites that bought the young Joseph, sold him off to an Egyptian captain. To cut the long story short, Joseph, who had a gift to interpret dreams, found himself before Pharaoh. In this dream, God revealed to Pharaoh the imminence of seven years of plenty, that would be succeeded by seven years of famine and lack. In other words, Egypt was about to experience a major deluge of harvest, the flow was about to rise in a very significant and magnanimous way. This bountiful flow would not be eternal. It would go for seven years, after which it would be followed by seven years of endemic drought.

Joseph, being a man of wisdom and strategy, was agile not only in interpreting the dream but in articulating a roadmap that detailed how the flow during the seven years of bounty could be captured and stored, in preparation for the seven years of famine. Furthermore, he was able to demonstrate competence in executing the plan, which saw Egypt emerge as a superpower during the time of famine. The strategy that Joseph developed centred around an astute of the flow.

"And now let Pharaoh look for a discerning and wise man and put him in charge of the land of Egypt. Let Pharaoh appoint commissioners over the land to take a fifth of the harvest of Egypt during the seven years of abundance. They should collect all the food of these good years that are coming and store up the grain under the authority of Pharaoh, to be kept in the cities for food. This food should be held in reserve for the country, to be used during the seven years of famine that will come upon Egypt, so that the country may not be ruined by the famine."

Genesis 41:33-36

Maximising the Flow

As we alluded to in earlier parts of the book, flows are forever in motion. This makes them somewhat perishable. The only way to transform a flow into an imperishable one is to convert the flow into stock by storing and preserving it for future use. Failure to do this will lead to a loss of the flow and thus minimising our gains and benefit from it. It takes strategy, insight, foresight, and tact to be able to maximise the flows of Africa to our ultimate benefit. One observable fact is that when the flow of something is abundant, people tend to value it less. However, when the flow of the same becomes scarce, its value increases. This was the reality in Egypt under Joseph's leadership. He possessed enough insight to value the flow of grain when other nations did not. He used this time to accumulate and store as much of that abundance as he could. He even went on to build store cities to accommodate the immeasurable harvest. This he did during a period when there was no famine in the land. Every nation had plenty for consumption, but only Egypt had the strategic foresight to store the abundance in preparation for an imminent famine.

When years of famine struck and the land was not bringing forth, Joseph unlocked the flows they had been stocking up and preserving for the previous seven years. His actions led to the most massive and magnanimous wealth transfer in ancient history. All through the power of maximising the flow through the power of strategy.

This kind of wisdom is needed on the continent. We need to move away from this culture of budget deficits and start creating surpluses especially during seasons when our resources are fetching favourable prices on global markets. Instead of consuming all we collect, we need to learn to build stocks and reserves from the flows of foreign currency, gold, oil, grain, diamonds, gas, platinum, bauxite, etc that we enjoy. This we must do with urgency but guided by a clear strategic focus. It is one of the ways that China employed as they positioned themselves for global dominance. Something that we need to do as well.

The Importance of Strategy

Strategy is a must-have discipline in the world we live in. If we are not looking to align ourselves to a future that is yet to manifest, we are simply denying our place and relevance in that future world. We weaken our position whenever we do not operate strategically as a continent. Part of my motivation in writing this book is to challenge us as a continent to prepare ourselves for the tide rising on the continent of Africa. Foresight allows us the opportunity to not only plan but to maximise the tide when it is at its peak. Strategic insight empowers us to align our infrastructure, talent, foreign policy, trade relationships, educational systems, and whatever else that will position us for growth and fruitfulness as a continent.

Strategic foresight also equips to effectively manage the ebbs and flow of the tide. The Word teaches us that *"For as long as the earth remains, seedtime and harvest, cold and heat, summer and winter, day and night shall not cease."* (Genesis 8:22 NKJV). Any leader operating in this world should know that the world operates on cycles. Good seasons will be followed by difficult ones.

Abundance will be followed by lack. So, it stands to reason that a wise leader will leverage current season in preparation for the opportunities that future seasons will bring. This kind of thinking is the product of strategic foresight.

From Joseph's model of managing and maximising flows, we learn some key realities about strategy, which if we embrace them, will radically transform our future as Africa. We have ascertained already that our challenge is not a resource challenge, neither is it a human capital challenge. Our challenges relate more to our inability to position ourselves appropriately considering our strengths, weaknesses, opportunities and threats. Ours is a strategy complexity.

1. Strategy Involves Shifting Our Focus from the Present to the Future

By its very nature, strategy is future focused. It relates to the moves and approaches taken to align to a future reality. The objective of this alignment is to maximise the opportunities inherent in the anticipated future. An example could be Africa's agricultural sector is set to become a $1 trillion industry by 2030. Leaders who possess strategic insight and whose strengths align to such an opportunity would be smart to begin realigning their policy frameworks, infrastructure, trade treatise, and financial systems to coincide with such a boom. Those who are less strategic, are likely to keep pursuing their expired and irrelevant economic development plans, which do not consider future opportunities.

Joseph shifted the focus of Egypt's economic policy from its conventional focus, to one that was aimed towards positioning Egypt for an uncertain tomorrow.

2. Strategy Improves Our Ability to Meet the Future with Readiness

Sound leaders also understand that the changes in flow create massive complexities and opportunities in the same breath. Analysts refer to these as shocks, abrupt changes caused by dramatic changes to the landscape. Joseph was able to discern such shocks in the future. This appreciation is what drove Pharaoh to seek out a wise and discerning man to whom they delegate the responsibility of executing an effective strategy. Such responsibility cannot be entrusted to incompetent people. A multi-trillion-dollar economy such as the one Africa is, must be in the hands of discrete men and women who have experience in dealing with such levels and degrees of complexity.

3. Strategy Must be Inclusive

Effective strategy execution requires a broad-based effort that includes all sectors from the grassroots going up to the visionary leader. If Joseph did not engage the commissioners and they were not monitored to ensure that they received the tax justly, and remitted it in full to the national treasury, the whole strategy would have been compromised. He needed buy-in and alignment from the lowest ranks to the highest.

Joseph's strategy stored food in multiple strategic locations across the land, close to the people and did not centralise it in one location. This improved collection of grain during times of plenty, and effective distribution during the seasons of famine. His strategy had to be inclusive for it to be effective.

4. Strategy Prepares Us to Manage Crisis Effectively

Joseph's strategy empowered Egypt to manage the crisis effectively. The land of Egypt was able to survive and thrive in crisis because of their preparedness and strategic response to the insight the Lord had given Joseph. Through effective strategic planning and execution, Egypt met with the famine from a place of readiness and advantage. They had been able to store the flow and build up strategic reserves and stocks when the flow was in abundance. This allowed them to unlock the flow during the period of famine, ensuring that none in Egypt perished as well as bringing prosperity to Egypt when the entire global economy was in a recession.

5. Strategy Demands Disciplined Execution

"Now in the seven plentiful years the ground brought forth abundantly. So, he gathered up all the food of the seven years which were in the land of Egypt, and laid up the food in the cities; he laid up in every city the food of the fields which surrounded them. Joseph gathered very much grain, as the sand of the sea, until he stopped counting, for it was immeasurable."
Genesis 41:47 - 49

A strategy is only as good as its implementation. The key to effective implementation of any strategy lies in discipline. During the years of plenty, Joseph's economic policy may have appeared misguided and misinformed to many. This did not deter its implementation and execution. He followed through with the plan and it paid off when it mattered most. He did not change strategy midway or after a few bountiful harvests. He stuck to the plan and executed it with discipline and a military-type rigour. Egypt went into a major agricultural drive during the years when the tide favoured them, and they stored the overflow with religious commitment. The routine was maintained for seven full years even though the results would only be felt and seen in the seven years of lack that followed.

Time for Spirit-Filled Leadership
"The plan seemed good to Pharaoh and to all his officials. [38] So Pharaoh asked them, "Can we find anyone like this man, one in whom is the spirit of God[a]?"
[39] Then Pharaoh said to Joseph, "Since God has made all this known to you, there is no one so discerning and wise as you. [40] You shall be in charge of my palace, and all my people are to submit to your orders. Only with respect to the throne will I be greater than you."
Genesis 41:37 – 40

It is never enough to have a plan that finds the approval of Pharaoh and his officials. There is a need for effective executors to oversee the plan and strategy. Thank God, Pharaoh had enough insight to appreciate Joseph's wisdom and character. He also registered that Joseph was a Spirit-filled man and that such a task was reserved for such a one, in whom the Spirit of the Lord is. Our continent needs leaders who are not only well educated, integral, exposed, experienced, and who possess exceptional expertise, they must also be Spirit-filled.

The complexities and opportunities that are coming in our direction are of such a colossal nature we need more than human intellect. We need Spirit-filled leadership in places of authority and influence. Africa's future needs men and women competence who are led by the Omniscient God into our illustrious future. The levels of wisdom and discernment required for our prophetic promise to become our future reality cannot be acquired even from the prime universities of our age. There is only one source for this degree and measure of competence, the Spirit of the Lord.

> " *There shall come forth a Rod from the stem of Jesse,*
> *And a Branch shall grow out of his roots.*
> *The Spirit of the Lord shall rest upon Him,*
> *The Spirit of wisdom and understanding,*
> *The Spirit of counsel and might,*
> *The Spirit of knowledge and of the fear of the Lord.*"
> **Isaiah 11: 1 -2**

The above portion of Scripture speaks of the Spirit of the Lord who rested on our Saviour as He was on the earth. The same Spirit of the Lord rests upon you and I. Notice how He is the Spirit of wisdom and understanding, counsel and might, knowledge and the fear of the Lord. Sadly, on the continent, we have restricted the Spirit of the Lord to our church experiences and yet the same Spirit of the Lord operated in people like Joseph, Deborah, Esther, Daniel, David, and Solomon. These individuals were used by God to turn the destinies of nations and economies around. Africa desperately needs the emergence of such leaders who carry the Spirit of the Lord.

I pray that we stop gambling with leadership responsibility by entrusting issues of our destiny to those who are not spiritually perceptive and cannot see into the future with clarity. For as long as the continent is led by those who are near-sighted and fail to see the threats and opportunities existing in the horizon, we will continually lose out on the many tides that God sends our way. Thank God that this is a peculiar generation of Africans.

PART IV

THE RISING TIDE

CHAPTER THIRTEEN

THE SHIP IS SAILING

—⌘—

"I have seen something else under the sun:
The race is not to the swift or the battle to the strong,
nor does food come to the wise or wealth to the brilliantor favor
to the learned; but time and chance happen to them all"

Ecclesiastes 9:11

The book of Ecclesiastes is filled with the wisdom of Solomon. It is the product of much reflection and assessment. In it, Solomon demonstrates an understanding of the forces that influence the world and the realities that we experience in this life. He makes some bold and audacious statements such as the one I have quoted. The Preacher is making us aware that many times we apply focus on things that do not determine the outcomes of our lives. In our human minds, races are for the swift, battles belong to the strong, bread to those who are wise, wealth is for the brilliant and favour follows the astute. The Preacher nullifies all these positions that we hold as concrete in our minds and narratives and establishes two major forces as supreme in the equation of life, time and chance.

The Power of Time and Opportunity

In act four of the epic play by William Shakespeare, Julius Caesar, Brutus sees an opportunity of a lifetime and chooses to engage Cassius to win his buy-in. Brutus felt that the events had conspired to their favour and it was the opportune moment to take on Octavius and Antony in battle. Brutus used the following quote in his pitch to Cassius,

> *'We at the height are ready to decline.*
> *There is a tide in the affairs of men*
> *Which, taken at the flood, leads on to fortune.*
> *Omitted, all the voyage of their life*
> *Is bound in shallows and in miseries.*
> *On such a full sea are we now afloat,*
> *And we must take the current when it serves,*
> *Or lose our ventures."*

Brutus speaks of the tide in the affairs of human existence. This imagery is drawn from the harbours where ships dock. When ships set sail and head out towards the sea, they generally rely on the high tides to thrust them on to the sea and possibly fuel them beyond what their efforts could have achieved. These tides are not under the control of man. No man determines when the tide will rise, and no one knows when the next one will come. However, a wise and smart captain will make haste to catch and leverage the tide that would have risen and set out on their journey. Brutus also acknowledges the momentary nature of the tide and the penalty that one pays when they miss it; they bound to the shallow waters and miseries, and they lose their ventures, or the opportunity altogether.

In the mind of Brutus, events had conspired in their favour and they would be wise to take advantage of this "Kairos" moment that had been presented to them. If not, there is no telling what possible outcome would befall them. Brutus appreciated the need for courage in the moment.

The Power of Courage

"And they went and came to Moses, and to Aaron, and to all the congregation of the children of Israel, unto the wilderness of Paran, to Kadesh; and brought back word unto them, and unto all the congregation, and shewed them the fruit of the land.

And they told him, and said, we came unto the land whither thou sentest us, and surely it floweth with milk and honey; and this is the fruit of it. Nevertheless, the people be strong that dwell in the land, and the cities are walled, and very great: and moreover, we saw the children of Anak there. The Amalekites dwell in the land of the south: and the Hittites, and the Jebusites, and the Amorites, dwell in the mountains: and the Canaanites dwell by the sea, and by the coast of Jordan.

And Caleb stilled the people before Moses, and said, let us go up at once, and possess it; for we are well able to overcome it.

But the men that went up with him said, we be not able to go up against the people; for they are stronger than we.

And they brought up an evil report of the land which they had searched unto the children of Israel, saying, The land, through which we have gone to search it, is a land that eateth up the inhabitants thereof; and all the people that we saw in it are men of a great stature. And there we saw the giants, the sons of Anak, which come of the giants: and we were in our own sight as grasshoppers, and so we were in their sight."

Numbers 13: 26 - 33

In Numbers 13, Moses sent twelve men into the land of Canaan on an espionage mission. Their deliverables were clear, assess the land, its landscape, the strength and population of its inhabitants, the nature of their settlements and cities, the fertility of their soils, and the state of their vegetation. They were to bring back a report and if possible, a sample of the fruit of the land. This they did, but when the twelve came back, two conflicting reports were delivered. Ten of the twelve had a report that differed from Joshua and Caleb. These reports were similar except for the contrasting conclusion. One group felt that attempting to take the land would be a suicide mission, while the other two had a different perspective. Let us look at Caleb's position on the matter.

"And Caleb stilled the people before Moses, and said, let us go up at once, and possess it; for we are well able to overcome it."
Numbers 13:30

Caleb's statement reveals a few key attitudes that I would like to highlight.

1. Unity

When the first report was given. Caleb silenced the people and spoke. His submission began with the words *"Let us..."* This demonstrates that he appreciated that the opportunity was not one to be selfish over and only consider his individual interest and effort. This was a window of opportunity for Israel as a whole and one that they would only possess as a people. Israel had to be of one mind and heart if they were to possess the land of promise that is flowing with milk and honey.

Africa needs to embrace this attitude that appreciates that we can never maximise the rising tide operating as a fragmented people. We need to unite in purpose, vision, and agenda. Thank God for blueprints like Agenda 2063, but we need to go beyond documents and charters and have that common and shared vision and purpose.

2. Urgency

Caleb appreciates a truth that we must also embrace in this season as Africa; the opportunity of a lifetime must be seized in the lifetime of the opportunity. The tide rises when God says, and not when we are ready. Ours is to respond with urgency when the tide rises.

As we speak, we are standing on the precipice of Africa's greatest spiritual and economic tide. Our generation is blessed to have been born for such a time as this. We must then choose to act with urgency. Perfect circumstances will never come our way, we will never be truly and fully prepared for the tide. We must rise and catch it while it is here.

3. Courage

Caleb does not deny the existence of the giants or the fortified cities in the land of promise. He just chose not to be deterred by them. He chose courage over fear. A similar attitude is what we need in all levels of leadership on the continent, from the continental level down to the regional, national, provincial, district, community, household and personal levels. We need to be as courageous as Africa.

Courage is what it will take to venture out to catch our rising tide. After all, the tide has our name on it, and we have come into our season. We must stop calculating our disadvantages and what works against us and appreciate that the times are ours and we must embrace the courage to align with what the times are presenting to us.

4. Proactivity

Caleb is not waiting for the nations within Canaan to present the land to them even though the land is theirs by Divine allocation and prophetic promise. He is coupling his courage with a proactive stance of going up at once. He seems to appreciate that God had given Israel a defining destiny moment, a portal in time that heaven has opened to allow humanity access to what God has promise. Caleb also seems to appreciate that this time window is not eternal. It is a do or die, now or never moment. Take it now or miss it. It was ride or die.

5. Belief

God will never promise us something He will not give us the capacity or opportunity to possess. The challenge many times lies with us. Our unbelief is oftentimes the self-sabotaging mechanism behind our stagnation and continual wandering in the wilderness of transition. As a continent we have been liberated from colonialism, we have conquered the odds that were stacked against us. We have been through civil conflict, and we have been successful at dislodging despots and warlords from seats of power. Our history testifies to what we can achieve if we are proactive, united, courageous and begin to function with urgency.

It is indeed our time as Africa.

Take-Two

"Now after the death of Moses the servant of the Lord, it came to pass, that the Lord spake unto Joshua the son of Nun, Moses' minister, saying,

Moses my servant is dead; now therefore arise, go over this Jordan, thou, and all this people, unto the land which I do give to them, even to the children of Israel.

Every place that the sole of your foot shall tread upon, that have I given unto you, as I said unto Moses.

From the wilderness and this Lebanon even unto the great river, the river Euphrates, all the land of the Hittites, and unto the great sea toward the going down of the sun, shall be your coast.

There shall not any man be able to stand before thee all the days of thy life: as I was with Moses, so I will be with thee: I will not fail thee, nor forsake thee.

Be strong and of a good courage: for unto this people shalt thou divide for an inheritance the land, which I sware unto their fathers to give them.

Only be thou strong and very courageous, that thou mayest observe to do according to all the law, which Moses my servant commanded thee: turn not from it to the right hand or to the left, that thou mayest prosper withersoever thou goest.

This book of the law shall not depart out of thy mouth; but thou shalt meditate therein day and night, that thou mayest observe to do according to all that is written therein: for then thou shalt

make thy way prosperous, and then thou shalt have good success.
Have not I commanded thee? Be strong and of a good courage;
be not afraid, neither be thou dismayed: for the Lord, thy God is
with thee whithersoever thou goest"

Joshua 1:1-9

Numbers 13 represents a missed opportunity that Israel had been afforded by God to possess the land. They were well able to, they just were not aware of it because they had been intimidated by the giants in the land. In His anger, the Lord caused them to wander for 38 years in the wilderness so that an entire generation which chose unbelief versus faith to die. Only Joshua and Caleb were preserved because they believed and as such, they were entrusted with the mandate to usher into Canaan a generation that did not know Egyptian bondage in any way.

After the thirty-eight years, another opportunity was availed to Israel under the leadership of Joshua. In Joshua chapter 1, God commissioned Joshua to go over the Jordan and go into to possess the land. Aware of the cost of a missed opportunity, Joshua would not gamble with this chance. Three times the Lord encourages him to be strong, bold, and of good courage. The fact is, it will take courage to rise from oblivion we are in and enter the space of prominence we are being called to.

Africa, it is time for us to step up, step out, and step into our prophetic destiny. The tide is rising, and we must confront our fears and ride the tide.

www.ingramcontent.com/pod-product-compliance
Lightning Source LLC
Chambersburg PA
CBHW050102210326
41519CB00015BA/3799